Teaching English as an International Language: Rethinking Goals and Approaches

Also published in
Oxford Handbooks for Language Teachers

ESOL: A Critical Guide
Melanie Cooke and James Simpson

The Oxford ESOL Handbook
Philida Schellekens

Teaching American English Pronunciation
Peter Avery and Susan Ehrlich

Success in English Teaching
Paul Davies and Eric Pearse

Doing Second Language Research
James Dean Brown and Theodore S. Rodgers

From Experience to Knowledge in ELT
Julian Edge and Sue Garton

Teaching Business English
Mark Ellis and Christine Johnson

Intercultural Business Communication
Robert Gibson

Teaching and Learning in the Language Classroom
Tricia Hedge

Teaching Second Language Reading
Thom Hudson

Teaching English Overseas: An Introduction
Sandra Lee McKay

Teaching English as an International Language
Sandra Lee McKay

How Languages are Learned (3rd edition)
Patsy M. Lightbown and Nina Spada

Communication in the Language Classroom
Tony Lynch

Teaching Young Language Learners
Annamaria Pinter

Exploring Learner Langauge
Elaine Tarone and Bonnie Swierzbin

Doing Task-based Teaching
Jane Willis and Dave Willis

Explaining English Grammar
George Yule

Teaching English as an International Language: Rethinking Goals and Approaches

Sandra Lee McKay

OXFORD
UNIVERSITY PRESS

OXFORD

UNIVERSITY PRESS

Great Clarendon Street, Oxford OX2 6DP

Oxford University Press is a department of the University of Oxford.
It furthers the University's objective of excellence in research, scholarship,
and education by publishing worldwide in

Oxford New York

Auckland Cape Town Dar es Salaam Hong Kong Karachi
Kuala Lumpur Madrid Melbourne Mexico City Nairobi
New Delhi Shanghai Taipei Toronto

With offices in

Argentina Austria Brazil Chile Czech Republic France Greece
Guatemala Hungary Italy Japan Poland Portugal Singapore
South Korea Switzerland Thailand Turkey Ukraine Vietnam

OXFORD and OXFORD ENGLISH are registered trade marks of
Oxford University Press in the UK and in certain other countries

ISBN: 978-0-19-437364-7

Printed in China

This book is printed on paper from certified and well-managed sources.

CONTENTS

ACKNOWLEDGMENTS

First and foremost, I would like to thank Henry G. Widdowson for his careful reading of the manuscript and constructive feedback. His insightful and direct comments helped me to rethink and reframe many aspects of the original manuscript. I am also grateful to Anne Conybeare, Julia Sallabank, and Cristina Whitecross for their support in the production of the book and to Kimberley Brown, her students, and an anonymous reviewer for their comments on the first draft of the book.

Many of the students and colleagues I have worked with in the United States and internationally also deserve recognition. The students I had in classes and lectures on English as an international language in the United States, Chile, Japan, Thailand, and Singapore helped me to conceptualize the framework for this book. I am particularly grateful to Ron Martin, who provided me with valuable information on the spread of English in Japan, and to Fay Purser, who offered an insightful analysis of how a textbook with United States cultural content might be viewed by Iranian students. I would also like to thank Gloria Salazar and Ana María Harvey of the Chilean Ministry of Education for sharing with me their perspectives on English teaching in Chile. Finally, I would like to thank my husband for his support of my international work and his patience during the writing and editing of this book.

An earlier treatment of the ideas discussed on page 88 appeared in McKay, S. L. (2001): 'Teaching English as an International Language: Implications for Cultural Materials in the Classroom.' *TESOL Journal* (Winter 2001) pp. 7–11.

The authors and publisher are grateful to those who have given permission to reproduce the following extracts and adaptations of copyright material:

The British Council for permission to reproduce extracts from *The Future of English?* by David Graddol.

David Crystal and Cambridge University Press for permission to reproduce extracts from *English as a Global Language* by David Crystal, 1997.

Sage publications India Pvt. Ltd, New Delhi, for permission to reproduce adapted extracts from chapter 8 (pp. 142–62) of 'Indian English: certain grammatical, lexical and stylistic features' by S. V. Parasher from *Sociocultural and Linguistic Aspects of English in India* © R K Agnihotri and A L Khanna, 1994. All rights reserved.

INTRODUCTION

Today in classrooms around the world young people and adults are involved in the study of English. Indeed this interest in the learning of English has increased to such an extent that English is now considered by many to be an international language. The central argument of this book is that the teaching and learning of an international language must be based on an entirely different set of assumptions than the teaching and learning of any other second or foreign language. The purpose of this book is to clarify these assumptions and advocate that they be considered in the design of English as an international language (EIL) teaching methods and materials.

There are a variety of factors that warrant a book that thoroughly examines the implications of the teaching and learning of EIL. These factors arise from three sources: the character of current users of EIL, the changes that have accompanied the spread of English, and the relationship that exists between culture and an international language.

Whereas today there are more native than non-native speakers of English, in the coming decades more and more users of EIL will be bilingual speakers of English who use English for a variety of specific purposes, often for cross-cultural communication. Some of these bilingual speakers will use English on a daily basis within their own country, at times for cross-cultural communication within their own borders. Others will have more restricted purposes in using English, often for accessing and sharing information. Given the great diversity of users of EIL, it is imperative we examine what goals and approaches in English language teaching (ELT) are appropriate for these various kinds of EIL users.

A second impetus for this exploration of the teaching of EIL comes from current changes in the language. The use of English as an international language has been brought about by the continuing spread of English. This spread has resulted in a variety of changes in English on grammatical, lexical, and phonological levels. Some contend that such changes will eventually lead to the varieties of English spoken today becoming mutually unintelligible. Hence, it is important to examine what kinds of changes are occurring in the use of English today and how these changes may affect intelligibility.

Finally, to be considered an international language, a language cannot be linked to any one country or culture; rather it must belong to those who use it. Hence, the typical relationship that exists between culture and language needs to be re-examined. This relationship needs to be examined with reference to three areas of language learning and teaching: the teaching of discourse competence, the use of cultural materials in the classroom, and the cultural assumptions that inform teaching methods. To the extent that appropriateness of language use is based on culturally influenced rules of discourse, the question of whose discourse rules to apply in the use of EIL will be problematic. Should those who use EIL be asked to acquire native speakers' standards of discourse use in both spoken and written interactions, or should they employ standards of appropriateness consistent with their own culture? The link between language and culture also has important implications for the choice of teaching materials. Currently, many ELT materials use cultural topics related to native English-speaking countries on the grounds that learning English should entail knowledge of native English-speaking cultures. Is such an approach appropriate in the teaching of an international language? Finally, to the extent that prevalent English teaching methodologies reflect the culture of learning of western English-speaking countries, if English is approached as an international language, whose culture of learning should be used? These are some of the central issues that arise in the teaching and learning of EIL and are examined in this text.

The book begins by defining the essential characteristics of an international language. The opening chapter, 'English as an international language', explores why English has developed as an international language, what factors might impede the continued spread of English, and what dangers are involved in the development of an international language. The chapter also includes current demographics regarding the number of English language users. These figures clearly demonstrate that in this century the number of bilingual users of English will far surpass the number of native speakers.

Chapter 2, 'Bilingual users of English', explores the pedagogical and research implications of the growing number of bilingual users of English. The chapter begins by examining the various meanings of the term 'native speaker' and argues that, given the difficulty of defining the term, native speaker competence should not be used as a standard in language learning and pedagogy. The chapter then describes various types of bilingual users of English and outlines some of the research that is needed to arrive at a fuller understanding of present-day bilingual users of EIL. I argue that to be productive this research cannot be based on native speaker models. The chapter ends by discussing the important role that bilingual teachers of English have in the teaching of EIL and points out the negative effects of using a native speaker model to assess such teachers.

Chapter 3, 'Standards for English as an international language', grapples with the complex issue of what standards should be promoted in the teaching of EIL on both a structural and discourse level. The first section of the chapter discusses the notion of standards in relation to EIL. Next, the chapter explores lexical innovation in specific varieties of English, noting how a good deal of this innovation has been accepted as a consequence of language change. This acceptance is contrasted with the debate that surrounds the issue of grammatical and phonological standards in the teaching of EIL. Finally, the chapter questions the use of native speaker models in the teaching of discourse competence in the use of EIL.

Chapter 4, 'Culture in teaching English as an international language', opens with a discussion of the relationship between language learning and culture and examines various rationales for giving attention to culture in language teaching. The chapter then delineates three primary sources of content for language teaching materials—cultural content from English-speaking countries, local cultural content, and international cultural content. Next the chapter explores the advantages and disadvantages of each type of content for the teaching of an international language and argues for a reflective approach to cultural content in EIL classes. The chapter ends with an examination of the cultural basis of discourse communities.

Chapter 5, 'Teaching methods and English as an international language', begins with a discussion of the concept of a culture of learning and challenges some of the generalizations made regarding so-called eastern and western cultures of learning. This is followed by an assessment of the appropriateness of a communicative language teaching (CLT) method for the teaching of EIL. The chapter ends by emphasizing the need to implement methods that are consistent with the local culture of learning.

Each chapter in the book ends with a list of suggested reading that provides the reader with sources for additional information on specific topics introduced in the chapter. There is also a glossary at the end of the book, containing terms that are central to an understanding of English as an international language.

This book is addressed to those who teach or will be teaching English to individuals who are learning the language alongside one or more other languages they speak to communicate with those from another culture and to participate in a growing global community. Because the book examines the assumptions that are involved in teaching an international language it will also be useful to individuals in English language curriculum and materials development and to those involved in English language acquisition research.

1 ENGLISH AS AN INTERNATIONAL LANGUAGE

Central to this book is the assumption that today English is an international language and that teaching it as such entails unique language teaching goals and approaches. We need to begin by examining the characteristics of an international language and how English has spread to become one.

Defining an international language

Number of users and official recognition

For some, an international language is equated with a language that has a large number of native speakers. In this sense, Mandarin, English, Spanish, Hindi, and Arabic, the five most widely spoken mother tongues in the world today, might be considered international languages. However, unless such languages are spoken by a large number of native speakers of other languages, the language cannot serve as a language of wider communication. It is in this sense, as a language of wider communication, that English is the international language *par excellence*. And in many instances it is a language of wider communication both among individuals from different countries and between individuals from one country. In this way, English is an international language in both a global and a local sense.

Crystal (1997) maintains that a language achieves global status when it develops a 'special role that is recognized in every country' (p. 2) and that this special status can be achieved either by making it an official language of the country or by a country giving special priority to English by requiring its study as a foreign language. (Today there are over seventy countries in which English has held or continues to hold special status, with many other countries giving English the special priority referred to by Crystal in which English is a required foreign language.) The countries that give special status to English are shown in Table 1.1, which also provides an estimate of the number of English speakers in these countries.

Kachru (1989) maintains that the various roles English serves in different countries of the world are best conceived of in terms of three concentric circles: (a) the *Inner Circle*, where English is the primary language of the

Table 1.1: Countries that give special status to English (from Crystal 1997: 57–60)

Territory	Population (1995)	Usage estimate	
American Samoa	58,000	L1	2,000*
		L2	56,000
Antigua & Barbuda (c)	64,000	L1	61,000
		L2	2,000
Australia	18,025,000	L1	15,316,000
		L2	2,084,000
Bahamas (c)	276,000	L1	250,000
		L2	25,000
Bangladesh	120,093,000	L2	3,100,000
Barbados (c)	265,000	L1	265,000
Belize (c)	216,000	L1	135,000
		L2	30,000
Bermuda	61,000	L1	60,000
Bhutan	1,200,000	L2	60,000
Botswana	1,549,000	L2	620,000
British Virgin Islands (c)	18,000	L1	17,000
Brunei	291,000	L1	10,000
		L2	104,000*
Cameroon (c)	13,233,000	L2	6,600,000
Canada	29,463,000	L1	19,700,000
		L2	6,000,0000
Cayman Islands	29,000	L1	29,000
Cook Islands	19,000	L1	1,000
		L2	2,000
Dominica	72,000	L1	3,000
		L2	12,000*
Fiji	791,000	L1	5,000
		L2	160,000
Gambia (c)	1,115,000	L2	33,000*
Ghana (c)	16,472,000	L2	1,153,000*

Table 1.1: continued

Territory	Population (1995)	Usage estimate	
Gibraltar	28,000	L1	25,000
		L2	2,000
Grenada (c)	92,000	L1	91,000
Guam	149,000	L1	56,000
		L2	92,000
Guyana (c)	770,000	L1	700,000
		L2	30,000
Hong Kong	6,205,000	L1	125,000
		L2	1,860,000
India	935,744,000	L1	320,000
		L2	37,000,000
Ireland	3,590,000	L1	3,400,000
		L2	190,000
Jamaica (c)	2,520,000	L1	2,400,000
		L2	50,000
Kenya	28,626,000	L2	2,576,000*
Kiribati	80,000	L2	20,000*
Lesotho	2,050,000	L2	488,000*
Liberia (c)	2,380,000	L1	60,000
		L2	2,000,000
Malawi	9,939,000	L2	517,000*
Malaysia	19,948,000	L1	375,000
		L2	5,984,000
Malta	370,000	L1	8,000
		L2	86,000*
Marshall Islands	56,000	L2	28,000*
Mauritius	1,128,000	L1	2,000
		L2	167,000*
Micronesia	105,000	L1	4,000
		L2	15,000*
Montserrat (c)	11,000	L1	11,000
Namibia	1,651,000	L1	13,000
		L2	300,000*
Nauru	10,000	L1	800
		L2	9,400
Nepal	20,093,000	L2	5,927,000*
New Zealand	3,568,000	L1	3,396,000
		L2	150,000

Table 1.1: continued

Territory	Population (1995)	Usage estimate	
Nigeria (c)	95,434,000	L2	43,000,000
Northern Marianas (c)	58,000	L1	3,000
		L2	50,000
Pakistan	140,497,000	L2	16,000,000
Palau	17,000	L1	500
		L2	16,300
Papua New Guinea (c)	4,302,000	L1	120,000
		L2	2,800,000
Philippines	70,011,000	L1	15,000
		L2	36,400,000
Puerto Rico	3,725,000	L1	110,000
		L2	1,746,000
Rwanda	7,855,000	L2	24,000*
St Kitts & Nevis (c)	39,000	L1	39,000
St Lucia (c)	143,000	L1	29,000
		L2	22,000
St Vincent & Grenadines (c)	112,000	L1	111,000
Seychelles	75,000	L1	2,000
		L2	11,000*
Sierra Leone (c)	4,509,000	L1	450,000
		L2	3,830,000
Singapore	2,989,000	L1	300,000
		L2	1,046,000
Solomon Islands (c)	382,000	L1	2,000
		L2	135,000
South Africa	41,465,000	L1	3,600,000
		L2	10,000,000*
Sri Lanka	18,090,000	L1	10,000
		L2	1,850,000
Suriname (c)	430,000	L1	258,000
		L2	150,000
Swaziland	913,000	L2	40,000*
Tanzania	28,072,000	L2	3,000,000
Tonga	100,000	L2	30,000*
Trinidad & Tobago (c)	1,265,000	L1	1,200,000
Tuvalu	9,000	L2	600
Uganda	18,659,000	L2	2,000,000*

Table 1.1: continued

Territory	Population (1995)	Usage estimate	
United Kingdom	58,586,000	L1	56,990,000
		L2	1,100,000
UK islands (Channel Is, Man)	218,000	L1	217,000
United States	263,057,000	L1	226,710,000
		L2	30,000,000
US Virgin Islands (c)	98,000	L1	79,000
		L2	10,000
Vanuatu (c)	168,000	L1	2,000
		L2	160,000
Western Samoa	166,000	L1	1,000
(now Samoa)		L2	86,000
Zambia	9,456,000	L1	50,000
		L2	1,000,000*
Zimbabwe	11,261,000	L1	250,000
		L2	3,300,000*
Other dependencies	30,000	L1	18,000
		L2	12,000
Total	2,024,614,000	L1	337,407,300
		L2	235,351,300

Notes: (c) indicates countries in which a large percentage of the population speaks a pidgin or creole variety of English.

An asterisk indicates a country in which no linguistic estimate is available. In these cases an indirect method of calculating totals has been used.

The category 'Other dependencies' consists of territories administered by Australia (Norfolk I., Christmas I., Cocos Is), New Zealand (Niue, Tokelan) and the UK (Anguilla, Falkland Is, Pitcairn I., Turks & Caicos Is).

country such as in Australia, Canada, the United States, and the United Kingdom; (b) the *Outer Circle*, where English serves as a second language in a multilingual country such as in Singapore, India, and the Philippines; and (c) the *Expanding Circle*, where English is widely studied as a foreign language such as in China, Japan, and Korea. The drawback of this categorization is that today many countries in what Kachru terms the Expanding Circle (e.g. Norway, Denmark, and the Netherlands) have many more English-speaking bilinguals than countries of the Outer Circle where English has an official status (e.g. the Gambia and Rwanda). Nevertheless, Crystal (1997) has found it helpful to use this model to provide an estimate of the current number of English speakers (see Figure 1.1).

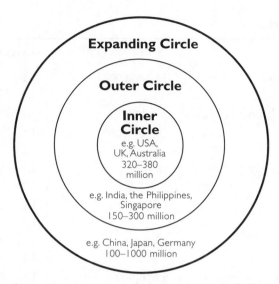

Figure 1.1: Kachru's categorization of countries in which English is used (from Crystal 1997: 54)

One of the advantages of Kachru's model is that it highlights the unique development of English in these three contexts (Graddol 1997). In the Inner Circle, English spread largely because of a migration of English speakers. In time each settlement developed its own national variety. On the other hand, the spread of English in the Outer Circle has occurred largely as a result of colonization by English-speaking nations. Here, two major types of linguistic development occurred. In some countries like Nigeria and India, where under colonial powers it developed as an elite second language, only a minority of the society acquired English. However, in other countries like Barbados and Jamaica, the slave trade had a significant impact on the variety of English spoken, resulting in the development of English-based pidgins and creoles. (Notice in Figure 1.1, some individuals contend that totals for English-based pidgin and creole speakers should be kept separate when estimating English language users.) The spread of English in the Expanding Circle is largely a result of foreign language learning within the country. As in the Outer Circle, the range of proficiency in the language among the population is broad, with some having native-like fluency and others having only minimal familiarity with English. However, in the Expanding Circle, unlike the Outer Circle, there is no local model of English since the language does not have official status and, in Kachru's (1992) terms, has not become institutionalized with locally developed standards of use.

Graddol (1997) contends that today in many parts of the world the status of English is shifting, with many countries in the Expanding Circle using it within the country as well as for international communication, as in countries of the Outer Circle. Graddol lists the following countries as in transition from an EFL context to an L2 context: Argentina, Belgium, Costa Rica, Denmark, Ethiopia, Honduras, Lebanon, Myanmar, Nepal, the Netherlands, Nicaragua, Norway, Panama, Somalia, Sudan, Suriname, Sweden, Switzerland, and the United Arab Emirates.

A variety of difficulties exist in getting an accurate count of the current number of English users. First, as Crystal (1997) points out, there is no single source of statistical information on totals of English language users of all countries in the world so estimates have to be made from a variety of sources. Second, how fluent an individual must be to be considered 'a user of English' is open to interpretation. This applies especially to those in the Expanding Circle, who are learning English as a foreign language. Finally, there are many varieties of the language, ranging from pidgins and creoles to various varieties of Standard English and, as was mentioned earlier, whether or not to include pidgin and creole speakers in estimates of English users is a subject of debate. Given these problems, Crystal (1997) contends that a conservative estimate of the number of speakers of English today with a native or native-like command of English would be 670 million. He continues that

> if we go to the opposite extreme, and use a criterion of 'reasonable competence' rather than 'native-like fluency,' we shall end up with a grand total of 1,800 million. A 'middle-of-the-road' estimate would be 1,200–1,500 million, and this is now commonly encountered. (Crystal 1997: 61)

Whereas the exact numbers of users of English is difficult to determine, it is clear that the number of individuals who have some familiarity with the language today is vast and growing. It is in the Expanding Circle where there is the greatest potential for the continued spread of English. Graddol (1997) points out that English is the most popular modern language studied in these countries, and cites the example of the Russian Federation, where 60 per cent of secondary school children study English as one of their foreign languages. However, the sheer number of speakers, as noted earlier, is not the defining characteristic of an international language. Other features need to be taken into account as well.

Features of an international language

Smith (1976) was one of the first to define the term 'international language', noting that an '*international* language is one which is used by people of different nations to communicate with one another' (p. 38). Elaborating on this definition, Smith makes several important assertions regarding the relationship of an international language and culture. These assumptions are that:

(a) its learners do not need to internalize the cultural norms of native speakers of that language
(b) the ownership of an international language becomes 'de-nationalized', and
(c) the educational goal of learning it is to enable learners to communicate their ideas and culture to others.

These assumptions are valid for the use of EIL in a global sense, where English is used by individuals to communicate with people of other countries. However, they need to be modified in reference to the use of EIL in a local sense, as occurs in many Outer Circle countries, where English is used as a language of wider communication within one country. Throughout the book, I will maintain, like Smith, that users of EIL whether in a global or local sense do not need to internalize the cultural norms of Inner Circle countries in order to use the language effectively as a medium of wider communication. Furthermore, when EIL is used by speakers from both Outer and Expanding Circle countries to communicate across borders, I agree that one of its main uses is to allow speakers to tell others about their ideas and culture. However, Smith's second assumption needs to be reframed as it relates to its local use in Outer Circle countries. Here the use of EIL has not become de-nationalized but rather its ownership has become re-nationalized. As we shall discuss in Chapter 3, it is this very process that has led to lexical and structural innovation in the varieties of English spoken in Outer Circle countries and caused concern about the lack of common standards in the current use of the language.

With regard to this distinction between global and local, Smith's notions concerning the relationship between an international language and culture warrant the following revisions.

1 As an international language, English is used both in a global sense for international communication between countries and in a local sense as a language of wider communication within multilingual societies.
2 As it is an international language, the use of English is no longer connected to the culture of Inner Circle countries.
3 As an international language in a local sense, English becomes embedded in the culture of the country in which it is used.
4 As English is an international language in a global sense, one of its primary functions is to enable speakers to share with others their ideas and culture.

Brutt-Griffler (2002) contends that four central features accompany the development of a world or international language. First, it is the product of the development of a world econocultural system, which includes the development of a world market and business community, as well as the development of a global scientific, cultural, and intellectual life. Second, it tends to establish itself alongside local languages in multilingual contexts composed of bilingual speakers. Third, unlike an elite *lingua franca*, it is not confined to the socioeconomic elite but is learned by various levels of society. Finally, an international language spreads not by speakers of that language migrating to other areas but rather by many individuals acquiring the language.

Today English exemplifies most of these features of an international language. To begin, few would question that presently it dominates a variety of economic and cultural arenas. In an issue of the *National Geographic* (Swerdlow 1999) devoted to the topic of the development of a global culture, the editor notes that today less than 30 per cent of Coca-Cola's income comes from the United States; that Toyota now sells over 1.3 million cars in the United States; that Nestlé now has food factories in 80 countries; and that more than 90 per cent of the top money-earning films in history are American productions. In other words, more and more products and trends from a variety of countries are reaching global markets. English facilitates this process and fuels its spread. Crystal (1997) offers further evidence of the domination of English in several important arenas including international relations, the mass media, international travel, international safety, education, and communications. We will discuss more fully the role of English in these arenas in the next section.

Demographic projections on the future users of English clearly demonstrate that it possesses Brutt-Griffler's second feature of a world language, namely that a world language establishes itself alongside of other languages. Thus Graddol (1999) uses demographic projections to show that the balance between native and non-native speakers of English will shift significantly in the next 50 years. He concludes that,

> based solely on expected population changes, the number of people using English as their second language will grow from 235 million to around 462 million during the next 50 years. This indicates that the balance between L1 and L2 speakers will critically change, with L2 speakers eventually overtaking L1 speakers.
> (Graddol 1999: 62)

Such projections support the point made earlier that one of the reasons for considering English an international language is the sheer number of people in the world who will have some familiarity with English. This shift reflects the use of English as a language of wider communication in a global sense for a great variety of purposes.

It is more difficult to demonstrate that English exemplifies the third feature of Brutt-Griffler's model of an international language, namely that it is learned by various levels of society and is not an elite *lingua franca*. There are few accurate figures to support exactly who is learning English. One can assume, however, that if English is a required subject in a country, school children will at least have some exposure to it. On the other hand, gaining a high level of proficiency in English typically requires more than the limited hours of instruction that generally occur in state school contexts and hence, those who want to attain a high level of proficiency in the language seek other means of learning, often in private institutes. This is certainly true in many Expanding Circle countries around the world today where there exists a huge industry of private programs to help individuals gain proficiency in English, often for exam and professional purposes. It also appears to be true in Outer Circle countries like India, in which many private schools, unlike state schools, are English medium, giving those who attend them more exposure to the language. (See Ramanathan (1999) for a discussion of educational institutional practices in India that keep lower income and lower caste groups from learning English.) Hence, it is difficult to support the notion that English is not in some sense an elite *lingua franca* since those who have more economic resources are often those who are able to attain greater proficiency in the language. The connection of English to economic resources and development is one we will return to shortly.

The final feature of Brutt-Griffler's model of an international language is that it spreads not through speaker migration but rather by many individuals in a speech community acquiring the language (what Brutt-Griffler terms 'macroacquisition'). Language spread by speaker migration results typically in the development of largely monolingual English-speaking communities (e.g. the United States, Australia, and New Zealand). Macroacquisition, on the other hand, in reference to English has occurred largely in Outer Circle countries but even, as was noted earlier, in some Expanding Circle countries. The result of this type of language spread, however, is not monolingualism but rather large-scale bilingualism.

As Brutt-Griffler (2002) points out, the fact that the spread of English today is primarily due to macroacquisition has two important implications. First, it means that the study of English as an international language must involve an investigation of bilingualism in both Outer and Expanding Circle countries, rather than of *language shift*, which often occurs when individuals move to Inner Circle countries. Second, because the current spread of English entails macroacquisition, the focus of investigation must be on bilingual English speech communities rather than on individual language learners. Both of these implications will be discussed in the next chapter.

There is one type of migration today that may be a significant factor in the continued growth of English, namely urban migration. Graddol (1997) notes that the most rapid urbanization today is taking place in the developing world where in Asia alone between 1994 and 2025 there is likely to be an increase of more than 20 per cent in the urban population. Graddol predicts that urbanization will have important effects on world languages since urban areas are typically the focus for linguistic change. They are also important points for language contact and diversity, and they encourage the growth of a middle class who become consumers of the global material culture. For Graddol,

> Urbanisation thus has important effects on language demography. New languages emerge, others change, some are lost. In the world's cities—the nexus for flows of people, goods and ideas—the spread of English will be felt first and most keenly; new patterns of English uses will arise amongst second-language speakers. But such cities will also form the foundation for other, potentially rival, lingua francas. (Graddol 1997: 27)

Urban migration then may have two effects on the spread of English. First, this process may encourage the acquisition of English, particularly among individuals with greater economic resources, thus further encouraging an economic split between English-knowing bilinguals and those who have little or no proficiency in the language. Second, urban centers may both encourage language change and stabilize this variation, resulting in new institutionalized varieties of English.

Various characteristics of English today, then, warrant it being considered as an international language, particularly in a global sense. Clearly it is a language being learned by more and more individuals as an additional language, it is central to a growing global economy, and it is the major language of a developing mass culture. How, then, has English acquired this international status?

Reasons for the spread of English

According to Crystal (1997), several geographical and historical factors as well as sociocultural ones led to the initial spread of English. During the nineteenth and twentieth centuries both British and American colonialism and the migration of English-speaking individuals to other areas were of central importance. In addition, by the beginning of the nineteenth century Britain had become the world's leading industrial and trading nation. Most of the innovations of the Industrial Revolution were of British origin, resulting in new terminology for technological and scientific advances. Hence, those who wanted to learn more about these innovations needed English both to understand the new terminology and to talk to English-speaking inventors and manufacturers. Similar developments were taking place in the United States, and by the end of the nineteenth century the United States had overtaken Britain as the fastest growing economy, producing many new inventions. Crystal summarizes the role of English during the nineteenth and early twentieth century as follows:

> The story of English throughout this period is one of rapid expansion and diversification, with innovation after innovation coming to use the language as a primary or sole means of expression. It is not possible to identify cause and effect. So many developments were taking place at the same time that we can only point to the emergence, by the end of the 19th century, of a climate of largely unspoken opinion which made English the natural choice of progress.
> (Crystal 1997: 75)

Crystal concludes that one of the primary reasons for the spread of English is that it has been in the right place at the right time. As he puts it,

> In the seventeenth and eighteenth centuries English was the language of the leading colonial nation—Britain. In the eighteenth and nineteenth centuries it was the language of the leader of the industrial revolution—also Britain. In the late-nineteenth century and the early twentieth it was the language of the leading economic power—the USA. As a result, when new technologies brought new linguistic opportunities, English emerged as a first-rank language in industries which affected all aspects of society—the press, advertising, broadcasting, motion pictures, sound recording, transport and communications.
> (Crystal 1997: 110–11)

Colonialism, speaker migration, and new technology developed in English-speaking countries were important in the initial spread of English, but what are the factors that are fueling its current spread and the macro-acquisition of the language within existing speech communities? In order to answer this question, it is useful to consider the current uses of English in various intellectual, economic, and cultural arenas. The following is a summary of some of these noted by Crystal (1997).

- International organizations: of 12,500 international organizations listed in the 1995–1996 *Union of International Associations' Yearbook,* approximately 85 per cent make official use of English.
- Motion pictures: in the mid-1990s, the United States controlled about 85 per cent of the world film market.

- Popular music: of the pop groups listed in *The Penguin Encyclopedia of Popular Music*, 99 per cent of the groups work entirely or predominantly in English.
- International travel: the United States is the leader in tourism earning and spending.
- Publications: more books are published in English than in any other language.
- Communications: about 80 per cent of the world's electronically stored information is in English.
- Education: in many countries English plays a significant role in higher education.

How then do such figures relate to the current demand for English learning and its role as an international language? To begin, consider the various implications of the fact that over 85 per cent of international organizations make some official use of English. Many of these organizations involve international relations, like the Association of South-East Asian Nations, the Council of Europe, and the North Atlantic Treaty Organization. Furthermore, some international organizations carry on their proceedings only in English. This is especially true in Asia and the Pacific where about 90 per cent of international bodies carry on their proceedings only in English. Many international scientific organizations as well as international sports associations also hold their proceedings only in English. Hence, English is the key as an international language in a global sense in enabling countries to discuss and negotiate political, social, educational, and economic concerns.

The widespread use of English in a variety of political and intellectual areas makes it imperative for any country wishing to access the global community for economic development to have access to it. Initially, English is often necessary for securing funds for development either through international organizations or private funding sources. When the aid has been granted, whether it involves public health issues, agricultural development, or advancements in transportation infrastructures, the dissemination of relevant information will most likely be in English. In these ways the language plays a key role in the economic development of a country.

English also dominates both the motion picture industry and popular music, two key components in what some term the development of a global culture, particularly among young people. Frequently those who decry the development of this global culture believe that its spread can be prevented by opposing the use of English. Yet it is not the language itself that is responsible; rather it is the highly profitable film and music industries, many based in the United States and other English-speaking countries. While English is not the cause of the spread of global culture, the fact that so much of popular mass video and music are in English makes the language enticing to many young people, often motivating them to study it.

Travel and tourism also fuel the current spread of English. Graddol (1997) points out that some estimates suggest that over 10 per cent of the world's labor force is now employed in tourist-related industries, and it is estimated that by the year 2006 there will be over 100 million new jobs in this area. As Graddol notes, international travel has a globalizing effect, promoting the need for a common language. Today this language is English. International airports around the world have essential information available in English and major international hotels have English-speaking staff available.

The significant role that English plays today in the storage and dissemination of information is another key factor in its continued spread. Crystal (1997), for example, points out that in the 1980s 85 per cent of biology and physics papers, 73 per cent of medical papers, and over 65 per cent of mathematics and chemistry papers were written in English, and contends that these percentages have increased significantly. Graddol (1997) points out that it is not just in scientific publishing but in book publishing as a whole that English is supreme. More books are published in English than in any other language (28 per cent) followed by Chinese (13.3 per cent), and then German (11.8 per cent). Graddol (1997) further notes that today over 84 per cent of the Internet servers are English medium followed by 4.5 per cent German and 3.1 per cent Japanese. These figures clearly demonstrate that one needs to know English today in order to access and contribute to both printed and electronic information.

Finally, access to higher education in many countries is dependent on a knowledge of English. Although it may not be the medium of instruction, accessing key information in a great variety of fields is often dependent on having reading ability in English. Furthermore, in many countries the sheer cost of higher education is encouraging universities to accept international students as a method of increasing revenues and in such circumstances English is frequently the medium of instruction. Thailand's Asian Institute of Technology is a case in point.

In sum, one of the primary reasons for the spread of English today is because it has such a variety of specific purposes (see Widdowson 1997). Knowledge of English is necessary for accessing many discourses at a global level from international relations to popular culture to academia. EIL, then, is not English for specific purposes in any narrow sense. Rather it is primarily because EIL is central to such a wide variety of specific purposes that it has gained global currency. Nevertheless, in spite of all this, we should note that there are factors that may impede the spread of EIL.

Factors that may impede the spread of English

One major factor that has impeded and will continue to impede the spread of English is that there is often little incentive for individuals, particularly in Expanding Circle countries, to acquire more than a superficial familiarity with the language. Martin (2000), for example, argues that one of the major reasons English will not spread widely in Japan is because of the low contact ratio between Japanese people and speakers of English. He points out that only 0.91 per cent of people living in Japan are non-Japanese residents, not all of whom are English speakers. Hence, there is little need in Japan to use English on a daily basis. (Whereas some Japanese do spend some of their life living abroad in English-speaking countries, there are more non-Japanese people living in Japan than Japanese people who live abroad.) Furthermore, Japan's limited use of English has had little impact on its ability to establish integral economic ties with regions all over the world, so there is not a strong economic incentive to learn English. In sum, there appears to be little need to use English among the Japanese population as a whole.

Another factor that may slow the spread of English is that it may lose its preferred status as a required foreign language, an important condition to assure its continued spread in Expanding Circle countries. Graddol (1997) lists several factors that may result in English not being a required foreign language. First, there may be competition from other languages, particularly on economic grounds. Current predictions suggest that by 2010 the most popular foreign language studied will be English, followed by Mandarin, Spanish, and Indonesian, all languages representing large potential markets. Second, in some countries the educational system, for internal political reasons, will need to cater for the needs of language minority groups within the country, thus requiring one of these languages to be taught rather than English. And finally, there may be political pressure to study the language of an adjacent country rather than English or a local *lingua franca*.

It is possible that technological factors could lead to a decline in the use of English as the creation of new technologies make translation more efficient and language compatibility on the Internet possible. Presently, as Crystal notes, the idea of a World Wide Web in which individuals can input data in their own language and expect any server to receive and display the data is a long way off. However, when the technological hurdles of this task are overcome, one of the incentives for learning and using English will be diminished. Graddol (1997) maintains that the Internet will increasingly serve local, cultural, and commercial needs and that this will result in the use of more languages on the Web. He points out that whereas today

80 per cent of the information stored on the World Wide Web is in English, as the use of computers spreads, it is predicted that English content may fall to 40 per cent of the total material.

National resources are another factor that may impede the spread of English. The macroacquisition of any language requires societal resources. Even if a country chooses to promote the learning of English, unless there is economic support to do this, it is not likely to spread. A comparison between Guatemala, Honduras, and Costa Rica demonstrates this. Whereas English is a required subject in all three countries, the fact that Guatemala spends only 1.7 per cent of its budget on education, Honduras 3.5 per cent, and Costa Rica over 33.3 per cent has had a significant impact on the spread of the language in these countries. Whereas Costa Rica is experiencing a growth in the learning of English, leading Graddol to include it as one of the countries that is shifting from an EFL to a L2 context, this is not occurring in either Guatemala or Honduras (McKay 1992).

The final, and perhaps most significant, factor is resistance to the spread of English arising from negative societal attitudes toward English and English-speaking nations. For example, in 1967 Tanzania made Swahili its sole official language, eliminating the official joint status of English. In the same year, Malaysia gave sole status to Malay as its official language. And in 1974, Kenya replaced English with Swahili as the official language. Such examples point to the fact that the spread of English may be seriously impeded by the belief that a nation's culture and sense of community may be compromised by it. We turn now to an investigation of some of the potentially negative effects of the development of EIL.

Negative effects of the spread of English

The main negative effects of the spread of English involve the threat to existing languages, the influence on cultural identity, and the association of the language with an economic elite. It has been argued that the spread of English reduces the role of existing languages, in some cases leading to their eventual extinction. In support of this claim, Swerdlow (1999), for example, points out that whereas today more than 6,000 languages exist, some linguists project that by the year 2100 the number of languages could drop to 3,000. Krauss (1992) predicts that the coming century may see the death of 90 per cent of the world's languages, many from Asian Pacific countries. Although not all of these languages are being replaced by English, there are many instances where it is replacing the mother tongue of a speech community. Such replacement is quite prevalent among immigrants to English-speaking countries. Veltman (2000), for example, clearly demonstrates the dramatic language shift to English that occurs in the case of United States immigrants.

However, it is not just in Inner Circle countries that a language shift to English is occurring. Gopinathan (1998), for example, points to the increasing number of households in Singapore in which English is the principal household language. Whereas in 1980, 7.6 per cent of Singaporeans used English as their principal household language, by 1990 this percentage had increased to 18.2. Nigeria is another country in which there is evidence that English is replacing other languages. Schaefer and Egbokhare (1999), for example, used oral questionnaire data to investigate the loss of African languages in rural southern Nigeria. They conclude that in this region, English is giving rise to the abandonment of indigenous, minority languages.

It has been argued that the primary reason for such a shift is the extensive promotion of English by English-speaking countries in the Inner Circle. One of the major exponents of this view is Phillipson (1992), who argues that the spread of English is a matter of deliberate policy on the part of core English-speaking countries to maintain dominance over *periphery countries*—in many cases developing countries. He has coined the term *linguistic imperialism* to describe a situation in which 'the dominance of English is asserted and maintained by the establishment and continuous reconstitution of structural and cultural inequalities between English and other languages' (p. 47).

However, to assume that the dominance of English is a function of the language itself, or its active promotion, is to oversimplify the complexity of the phenomenon of language spread. Many individuals learn English not because they wish to become bilingual or have a love of the language, or even because it is 'sold' to them by a growing private industry, but rather because they want access to such things as scientific and technological information, global economic trade, and higher education. Knowing English makes such access possible. Indeed Kachru contends that 'knowing English is like possessing the fabled Aladdin's lamp, which permits one to open, as it were, the linguistic gates to international business, technology, science and travel. In short, English provides linguistic power' (1986: 1).

There is a variety of evidence to suggest that a belief in the power of English is widespread. Chew (1999), for example, argues that the spread of English within Singapore is the conscious choice of Singaporeans who view its use as key to their economic survival. She points out that whereas some Singaporeans are concerned that the widespread adoption of English will lead to a loss of ethnic identity and Asian values, many value the material and other rewards that knowledge of the language can bring. As she puts it, among parents there has been a pragmatic realization that 'lack of a command in English would mean the continued marginalisation of their children in a world that would continue to use the language to a greater degree. It would also deny them access to the extensive resources available in English—resources which have developed as a consequence of globalisation' (Chew 1999: 41).

Bisong (1995) challenges Phillipson's theory of linguistic imperialism as it relates to his own country, Nigeria. He notes that presently many Nigerian parents send their children to international schools in which they are sure they will learn English, and maintains that it is important to consider why a parent would make such a decision. For Bisong, a parent does so not because of coercion but rather

> in the secure belief that her child's mother tongue or first language is not in any way threatened. There is no way three or four hours of exposure to English in a formal school situation could possibly compete with, let alone threaten to supplant, the non-stop process of acquiring competence in the mother tongue.
> (Bisong 1995: 125)

Bisong concludes by pointing out that Nigerians learn English for pragmatic reasons and that Nigerians are

> sophisticated enough to know what is in their interest, and that their interest includes the ability to operate with two or more linguistic codes in a multilingual situation. Phillipson's argument shows a failure to appreciate fully the complexities of this situation.
> (Bisong 1995: 131)

As suggested above, the replacement of local languages with English raises important issues regarding the relationship between language and cultural identity. It has been argued that the spread of English has led to local traditions being replaced by a largely western-influenced global culture. Indeed today one can witness the celebration of Halloween in Chile, the lighting of Christmas trees in Japan, and the sending of Valentine's Day cards in India. To some, all of this is a direct result of the spread of English. Again, however, it is not the language itself that is the culprit. Rather it is global communication, western-dominated mass media, the economic benefits that various celebrations bring through the marketing of greeting cards and gifts, and a desire among many young people around the world to be part of a global culture that have brought about these developments.

The relationship between the spread of English and cultural identity has also been raised in relation to encouraging a negative view of non-western cultures. Here colonialism is perceived as being instrumental in promoting the spread of English and with it the devaluing of non-western cultures. The Kenyan writer, Ngũgĩ, for example, in his book *Decolonizing the Mind: The Politics of Language in African Literature*, asserts that one of the most significant areas of domination promoted by colonialism 'was . . . the control, through culture, of how people perceived themselves and the world' (1986: 16). For Ngũgĩ, this mental control has been achieved primarily by colonial powers devaluing the culture of the local people and striving to replace their language with that of the colonizer. Kubota (1998) raises a similar concern with reference to Japan but suggests that a negative view of non-westerners is promoted not by colonialism but by English teaching itself. She maintains that one way English exerts influence in Japan is through the images that English textbooks present of language, culture, race, and ethnicity. Often what is represented in these textbooks is the superiority of native speakers of English and their culture. But once again it is not the English language itself nor its widespread acquisition that is the cause of such negative stereotyping. Rather the blame must rest with those who disseminate books and ideas that portray such negative images.

Finally, many concerns are raised in relation to the negative economic repercussions of the spread of English. One of the primary concerns in this regard is the strong relationship between economic wealth and proficiency in the language, and the role that language education policy and practices play in promoting this. Tollefson (1991), for example, notes that because English is typically acquired in school contexts, this situation can lead to significant social inequalities. As he puts it,

> those people who cannot afford schooling, who do not have time to attend school, who attend substandard programmes, or who otherwise do not have access to effective formal education may be unable to learn English well enough to obtain jobs and to participate in decision-making systems that use English. Because education is a major concern of the state, this fundamental shift in the manner of acquisition means that state policies play a decisive role in determining who has access to the institutions of the modern market and therefore to political power. This shift to school-based language learning is a worldwide phenomenon, and so language policy plays an important role in the structure of power and inequality in countries through the world.
> (Tollefson 1991: 6)

My work in Durban, South Africa (Chick and McKay 2001) supports Tollefson's concern regarding the relationship between social inequalities and English language learning. Whereas South Africa has an official language policy that supports the development of multilingualism and multiculturalism in society in general, language practices that promote the use of English in some communities and not in others are developing a select English language proficiency among the elite. Parents in the Durban area who can afford to do so are sending their children to former white and Indian schools in the community. Since these schools are English medium whereas those in the former black townships are largely Zulu medium, there is a growing split between those who know English and have access to greater economic resources and those who do not. Indeed, to me one of the major concerns that must be raised is the growing relationship between English proficiency and economic resources. In many countries around the world English is being learned only by those who can afford instruction in it. Not being able to afford such instruction can close many doors, particularly with regard to accessing higher education.

Clearly an assessment of the negative effects of the spread of English needs to be based on a full recognition of its complexity. Its spread cannot be viewed simply as the result of imposition by colonial powers or Inner Circle countries, but rather as a complex process brought about both by those who actively promote the language and those who consciously choose to learn it. At the same time, it is important to emphasize that the ability to develop English proficiency is greatly enhanced when the resources are available to pursue its study. In many cases English is spreading primarily among those with greater economic resources, thus contributing to social inequalities. Hence, it is important for educators to take a critical view and to recognize, as Pennycook points out, that in many ways 'English . . . acts as a gatekeeper to positions of wealth and prestige both within and between nations, and is the language through which much of the unequal distribution of wealth, resources, and knowledge operates' (1995: 54).

Summary

This chapter has examined the development of EIL. Central to the chapter is the notion that although an international language must be widely spoken and recognized, this is not a sufficient condition to define a language as such. Rather, an international language is one that is no longer linked to a single culture or nation but serves both global and local needs as a language of wider communication. Another important feature of an international language is that it develops alongside other languages. Hence, in *second language acquisition* (SLA) research and in designating teaching goals and designing course materials, it is important to consider how English is used within specific bilingual communities.

This chapter has also examined what factors have led to the spread of English and what factors may impede its continued growth. Although many seem to believe that there is no question that the use of English will continue to grow, as noted above various factors could impede it. These include new translation technology, incentives for learning regional languages rather than an international language, a lack of economic resources to promote its instruction, and negative attitudes toward the language and the cultures and nations with which it is associated. Finally, the chapter emphasized that the spread of English has both positive and negative implications. Whereas an international language can contribute to greater efficiency in the sharing of information, to economic development, and to cross-cultural communication, there are also significant dangers in this process. Perhaps the most serious of these is the promotion of social inequalities based on a lack of access to instruction in the language. We turn now to an investigation of how English is used by bilingual speakers. Central to Chapter 2 will be an examination of the validity of using native speaker norms in the determination of teaching goals for bilingual users of English, in undertaking second language acquisition research, and in the professional assessment and hiring of teachers.

Further reading

General accounts of English as an international language

Crystal, D. 1997. *English as a Global Language.* Cambridge: Cambridge University Press.

Graddol, D. 1997. *The Future of English.* London: The British Council.

Graddol, D. 1999. 'The decline of the native speaker.' *AILA Review* 13: 57–68.

On the causes and effects of the spread of English

Brutt-Griffler, J. 2002. *English as an International Language.* Clevedon: Multilingual Matters.

Pennycook, A. 1995. 'English in the world/The world in English' in Tollefson, J. W. (ed.): *Power and Inequality in Language Education.* Cambridge: Cambridge University Press: 34–58.

Phillipson, R. 1992. *Linguistic Imperialism.* Oxford: Oxford University Press.

Tollefson, J. W. 1991. *Planning Language, Planning Inequality.* London: Longman.

2 BILINGUAL USERS OF ENGLISH

As was pointed out in Chapter 1, there is little question that in the course of this century the number of L2 users of English will continue to grow, far exceeding the number of native speakers. The purpose of this chapter is to distinguish various types of L2 speakers and delineate contexts in which English is being used primarily as an international language. This will lay the groundwork for subsequent chapters that examine what type of pedagogy is appropriate for contexts in which English is used primarily as an international language.

In this chapter and throughout the book I will use the term *bilingual users of English* to describe individuals who use English as a second language alongside one or more other languages they speak. Although Jenkins (2000) includes in her use of the term 'bilingual English speaker' both native and non-native speakers, in my use of the term 'bilingual users of English', I am excluding native speakers of English who speak other languages. I do so because whereas most native speakers use English for all of their communicative needs, bilingual users of English typically use English for more restricted and formal purposes.

Jenkins also distinguishes bilingual English speakers from 'non-bilingual English speakers'. She uses the latter term to describe those individuals with limited English proficiency whose English has 'progressed to the level at which it serves their particular international communicative need' (p. 10). Because there is a continuum in English language proficiency, making it difficult to draw a clear line between two terms, I will use the term 'bilingual users of English' to describe a wide range of English proficiency. However, I will emphasize throughout the book that there is a tremendous variety in language ability among bilingual English speakers, with some speaking English like native speakers and others having limited English proficiency that meets their particular communicative needs.

Traditionally L2 pedagogy and research have been dominated by the assumption that the goal of bilingual users of English is to achieve native-like competence in English. However, for those individuals who use English essentially as a language of wider communication alongside one or more other languages they speak, achieving native-like competence is often not necessary or desired. Hence, one goal of this chapter is to argue that a native speaker norm in English language research and pedagogy is not relevant to many contexts in which English is used as an international language. In order to evaluate the validity and appropriateness of a native speaker norm, the chapter begins with a discussion of what is meant by the term 'native speaker'. This is followed by an analysis of various types of present-day bilingual users of English. The purpose of this discussion is to demonstrate the wide diversity of uses of EIL among bilinguals.

The third section of the chapter examines how the native speaker fallacy has informed a good deal of SLA research, and argues that the assumption that all bilingual users want to achieve native-like competence restricts the applicability of much of it. I then discuss some of the areas of research that are needed in reference to EIL. In the final section, the native speaker fallacy is examined as it relates to present-day bilingual teachers of English. Various types of bilingual teachers are described in order to highlight their advantages in particular ELT contexts.

Defining a native speaker

The term 'native speaker of English' has been subjected to a great variety of interpretations. For some, an essential feature of a native speaker is that English must be the first language learned; for others, to be a native speaker involves the continued use of English in that person's life; for still others, being a native speaker assumes a high level of competence in English.

The *Longman Dictionary of Applied Linguistics* (Richards, Platt, and Weber 1985: 188) defines a native speaker as a 'person considered as a speaker of his or her native language'. A native language is then defined as the language that 'a person acquires early in childhood because it is spoken in the family and/or it is the language of the country where he or she is living' (ibid.: 188). The definition continues that whereas a native language is typically the first language children acquire, there are exceptions: for example, children can acquire some knowledge of a language from a nurse or older relative but later acquire another language that they consider their native language. This exception to the initial definition suggests that first exposure to a language is not sufficient for it to be considered someone's native language; rather there exists some level of competence that is necessary in defining a native speaker.

Davies (1991) makes an important addition to the idea that a native language is the first learned language in which one achieves a high degree of competence and linguistic intuition. He notes that being a native speaker

> is only partly about naïve naturalness, that is about not being able to help what you are, it is also, and in my view more importantly, about groups and identity: the point is of course that while we don't choose where we come from we do have some measure of choice of where we go to. Difficult as it is, we can change identities, . . . we can join new groups.
> (Davies 1991: ix)

Davies's statement suggests that changing group identity may lead to becoming a native speaker of another language. Many would agree with Davies that the notion of identity is related to the concept of a native speaker. However, if one accepts the idea, discussed in Chapter 1, that an international language is one that is de-nationalized, then relating the two becomes highly problematic. One could even argue that an essential feature of an international language is that identifying with a group that speaks it is not necessary for the development of native-like competence.

In addition to the criteria of first learned language, native intuition, and group identity as central to a definition of a native language, Tay (1982) adds the criterion of continued use. She argues that a native speaker who is not from an Inner Circle country is

> one who learns English in childhood and continues to use it as his dominant language and has reached a certain level of fluency. All three conditions are important. If a person learns English late in life, he is unlikely to attain native fluency in it; if he learns it as a child, but does not use it as his dominant language in adult life, his native fluency in the language is also questionable; if he is fluent in the language, he is more likely one who has learned it as a child (not necessarily before the age of formal education but soon after that) and has continued to use it as his dominant language.
> (Tay 1982: 67–8)

Certainly language use is related to proficiency but there is no causal relationship between the two. An individual could conceivably use English in childhood and not attain a high level of proficiency in the language even when it is the dominant language of the home. Indeed, some Inner Circle educators decry the lack of English proficiency among so-called native speakers. On the other hand, an individual's use of English may be restricted, but nonetheless he or she could achieve a high level of proficiency in the language through personal motivation and effort.

Rampton (1990) summarizes what he believes are features most individuals associate with being a native speaker of a language.

1 A particular language is inherited, either through genetic endowment or through birth into the social group stereotypically associated with it.
2 Inheriting a language means being able to speak it well.
3 People either are or are not native/mother-tongue speakers.
4 Being a native speaker involves the comprehensive grasp of a language.
5 Just as people are usually citizens of one country, people are native speakers of one mother tongue.
    (Rampton 1990: 97)

Whereas it is difficult to accept the notion that a native language is inherited by genetic endowment, the other features, particularly the idea that one can be a native speaker of only one language are widely held. Rampton disputes each of these features of a native speaker, arguing that an individual can belong to more than one social group and hence acquire one or more languages in early childhood. In this way, he or she could be a native speaker of more than one language. In addition, as just pointed out above, not all individuals who learn a language from birth are necessarily fluent speakers. Most importantly for Rampton, since membership in a group can change over time, one can change one's native language.

Because of the difficulty of arriving at a clear definition of the term 'native speaker', recently there has been a growing challenge to the relevance and usefulness of the term. Rampton advocates replacing the term with the concept of 'expertise'. In his view this concept has the following advantages:

1 Although they often do, experts do not have to feel close to what they know about. Expertise is different from identification.
2 Expertise is learned, not fixed or innate.
3 Expertise is relative. One person's expert is another person's fool.
4 Expertise is partial. People can be expert in several fields, but they are never omniscient.
5 To achieve expertise, one goes through processes of certification, in which one is judged by other people. Their standards of assessment can be reviewed and disputed.
    (Rampton 1990: 98–9)

Whereas there are clear advantages to using the concept of expertise rather than native speaker status as a basis for judging language proficiency, this leaves open the question of how to assess expertise.

Cook (1999) points out that the general meaning of the term 'native speaker' is a monolingual person who still speaks the language learned in childhood. However, since individuals who speak English will increasingly be using English alongside other languages, Cook suggests using the term 'L2 user' as distinct from 'L2 learner'. Pakir (1999) makes a similar suggestion, referring to such individuals as 'English-knowing bilinguals'. One of the primary benefits of using the terms 'L2 user' or 'English-knowing bilingual' is that they emphasize the idea that individuals who use English along with another language are not in the process of learning English. Rather they have available to them two or more languages that often serve different purposes. Cook (1999) refers to those who have more than one language available to them as 'multicompetent language users'. The advantage of using terms that highlight an individual's bilingualism is that fluency can be seen in reference to an individual's complete linguistic repertoire rather than assessed as a factor of his or her knowledge of one particular language.

What does a recognition of the problems of defining native speakers, coupled with the dramatic growth in the number of bilingual English users, suggest for traditional views of learning the language? First, if, as the previous discussion has shown, there is no satisfactory characterization of the term 'native speaker', then it is foolish to accept the construct of native speaker as a model of competence. Yet this is clearly what has often been done in SLA research and ELT pedagogy. As Graddol notes, one of the primary drawbacks of using the term 'native speaker' is that

> it locates the 'native speaker' and native-speaking countries at the centre of the global use of English and, by implication, the source of models of correctness, the best teachers and English-language goods and services consumed by those in the periphery.
> (Graddol 1997: 10)

He proposes that the three concentric circles shown in Figure 1.1 be reconfigured as three overlapping circles as shown in Figure 2.1. Reconfiguring the relationship in this way challenges the traditional view of affording special status to English speakers of the Inner Circle both for determining standards of use and defining language pedagogy. As Graddol notes, Figure 2.1 also illustrates the manner in which the center of gravity will likely shift toward second and first language speakers during the twenty-first century.

Second, if as was demonstrated in Chapter 1, the use of EIL will be predominantly among bilingual users of English, it is important to examine the various ways in which bilinguals make use of English within their full linguistic repertoire rather than compare them to native speakers. As an initial step in that direction, we turn now to a consideration of

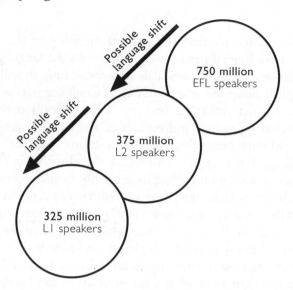

Figure 2.1: Model of the changing patterns in the use of English (from Graddol 1997: 10)

English language use within various multilingual communities. Such a discussion demonstrates both the diversity of contexts of English language use today and the inadequacies of accepting the notion that the goal of English learning, particularly when English is used as an international language, is to achieve native-like competence.

Bilingual users of English

In Chapter 1 we discussed the way in which the current spread of English as an international language has come about largely as a result of macro-acquisition within existing speech communities, resulting in a situation of additive bilingualism or multilingualism. The growth in numbers of bilingual speakers of English within Outer and Expanding Circle countries highlights the need for ELT professionals to investigate the language use patterns of speech communities that use English alongside other languages. Graddol aptly summarizes the issue in the following manner.

> But a full understanding of the role of English in a world where the majority of its speakers are not first-language speakers requires an understanding of how English relates to the other languages which are used alongside it. The European concept of bilingualism reflects an idea that each language has a natural geographical 'home' and that a bilingual speaker is therefore someone who can converse with monolingual speakers from more than one country. The ideal bilingual speaker is thus imagined to be someone who is like a monolingual in two languages at once. But many of the world's

bilingual or multilingual speakers interact with other multilinguals and use each of their languages for different purposes: English is not used simply as a 'default' language because it is the only language shared with another speaker; it is often used because it is culturally regarded as the appropriate language for a particular communicative context.
(Graddol 1997: 12)

What is needed then is a much more robust picture of how bilinguals in various communities around the world use English for specific communicative purposes.

Graddol argues that languages in a multilingual context often have a hierarchically ordered status as shown in Figure 2.2. At the base of the pyramid are languages that are typically used with family and friends for informal purposes. These are generally geographically based and often the first language a child acquires. Higher up the pyramid are languages used in more formal and public domains which, in Graddol's terms, have a more extensive territorial reach. These are often used in primary education and in local news reporting and commerce. Finally, at the top of the pyramid are languages used in official administration and higher education, which are typically languages of wider and international communication. It is here, of course, that English is gaining dominance. The taper of the pyramid illustrates the fact that fewer languages are used for purposes of wider communication than for informal purposes. Within multilingual

Figure 2.2: The world language hierarchy (from Graddol 1997: 13)

countries, not all individuals will be fluent in one, or more, of the languages at the top of the pyramid. In fact many of the world's population never require or have access to this group. However, Graddol contends that as a result of changing patterns of international communication more and more people in the world will learn languages at the top of the pyramid, an assertion which, as we discussed in Chapter 1, may be true primarily for those with greater economic resources.

For purposes of delineating individual uses of the 'big languages', it may be helpful to contrast the world language hierarchy shown in Figure 2.2 with a personal language hierarchy shown in Figure 2.3 in which the big languages exist at the top of an inverted pyramid. The reason for doing so is to emphasize the fact that in terms of individual use, the big languages have, as Graddol notes, a wider territorial reach. Hence, languages at the top of the pyramid can reach more people, making cross-cultural communication possible.

In order to demonstrate the great diversity of ways in which bilingual users of English make use of the language, we turn now to an examination of present-day bilingual users, referring to the three concentric circles in Figure 1.1. It is important to emphasize, however, that although some comparisons can be made between bilingual users within these three circles, countries are unique in how they make use of English. Furthermore, within any one country there exists a variety of speech communities that use the language in different ways.

Bilingual users of English in Inner Circle countries

Bilingual users of English in Inner Circle countries are typically first or second generation immigrants. In many instances, particularly among immigrants or children of immigrants, English is used in all public

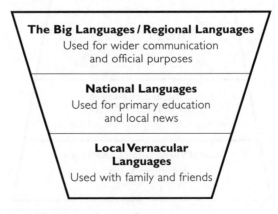

Figure 2.3: Personal language hierarchy

domains and even in some instances in the private domains of family and friends. (See Zentella (2000) for a description of various communication patterns in bilingual homes in the United States.) In this way English can serve most, or even all, of the purposes in an individual's personal language hierarchy. In contrast to Outer Circle contexts, in which codeswitching often occurs in public domains, codeswitching in Inner Circle contexts typically occurs within informal domains among family and friends. More importantly, bilingual users of English in Inner Circle contexts interact with native speakers of English on a daily basis.

There are, then, important differences that distinguish bilingual users of English in Inner Circle countries from those in other countries. First, such speakers acquire English because of speaker migration rather than the process of macroacquisition that occurs in Outer and Expanding Circle countries. Second, for many of these bilinguals, English is the preferred language for most, or all, of their personal language hierarchy. Third, many of the speakers come to identify with the culture of the Inner Circle country and become members of English-only speech communities. Finally, for many of these speakers, particularly the younger ones, English is learned as a replacement for their other language or languages rather than an addition to their existing linguistic repertoire.

Bilingual users of English in Outer Circle countries

In Outer Circle countries, the linguistic repertoire of bilingual users of English can be a highly complex phenomenon, with each language serving a particular purpose. Sridhar (1996a), for example, cites Pandit's (1978) example of the linguistic life of a spice merchant in India.

> A Gujarati spice merchant in Bombay uses Kathiawadi (his dialect of Gujarati) with his family, Marathi (the local language) in the vegetable market, Kacchi and Konkani in trading circles, Hind or Hindustandi with the milkman and at the train station, and even English on formal occasions. Such a person may not be highly educated or well versed in linguistic rules, but knows enough to be able to use the language(s) for his purposes.
> (Pandit 1978: 79, as cited in K. K. Sridhar 1996a: 50)

Myers-Scotton (1993) has proposed a Markedness Model to account for such shifts in bilinguals' use of codes. According to this theory, speakers 'exploit the possibility of linguistic choices to convey intentional meaning of a socio-pragmatic nature' (p. 57). For Myers-Scotton, code choices are an index of the rights and obligations that exist among participants in a given interaction. The 'unmarked choice' is the code that would typically be used in a particular community for a specific type of interaction; the 'marked choice' is the unexpected code in a particular situation. In order to clarify how the use of English can be both the unmarked and the marked choice in the repertoire of multilingual users in Outer Circle countries, it is useful to examine some specific contexts and interactions.

In South Africa, Chick (1996) has studied native Zulu-speaking students communicating with their professors at the University of Durban, Natal. In this public education context, English is clearly the unmarked code. Chick and McKay (2001) have also shown how English in South Africa is the unmarked code in a growing number of high schools in the Durban area, with the mother tongue being used only in restricted school contexts like the playground and lunchroom. In Singapore, McKay (2000a) highlights how, throughout the educational system, English is the unmarked code.

English, however, can also be the marked choice in multilingual English-using Outer Circle countries. Myers-Scotton (1993) points out that in Kenya, Swahili is typically the unmarked choice between strangers. She cites the following example, in which the young man uses English, a marked choice, as a way of challenging the expected relationship between a conductor and passenger. The young man makes his sarcastic answer even more offensive to the conductor by speaking in English, a language typically used in Kenya by an individual who has more prestige speaking to one with less power. (In the following examples, all of the italicized phrases are in English whereas the phrases in regular type are in Swahili.)

Example 1
>   **Conductor** (to a smartly dressed young man who is standing) Have you already paid the fare?
>   **Young man** *Don't you see that I am in a position in which I can't take something from my pocket?*
>   **Same young man** (adding in Swahili) You people fill the bus with people and you don't have enough seats.
>   **Conductor** This is the property of the owner or the government. It isn't your property so that you should make your bad play [comment]. There are people with [the bus] who know English, but they show us respect.
>   (Myers Scotton 1993: 108–9)

This exchange illustrates that multilingual speakers in Outer Circle countries have a rich linguistic repertoire they can use to define and challenge their role relationship with others.

Typically, however, English in Outer Circle countries is the unmarked code in more formal contexts, being used as a language of wider communication between linguistic and cultural groups. Hence, unlike bilingual users of English in Inner and Expanding Circle countries, often bilingual users in Outer Circle countries use English as a language of wider communication both within their own country and with countries of the Inner and Expanding Circle. And, as we shall see in the next chapter, this internal use of English has led many Outer Circle countries to develop linguistic and pragmatic standards that differ from those of Inner Circle countries.

In some Outer Circle countries, bilingual users are beginning to use English in more and more domains. Hence, English has penetrated to the lower levels of their personal language hierarchy, being the unmarked choice even in some informal contexts. This is occurring in countries like Singapore and South Africa, where English is being promoted within multilingual and multicultural schools and used widely in the mass media. (See McKay (2000a) for a comparison of the promotion of English within these two countries.) In such instances, the pattern of use can be quite similar to that of bilingual immigrants in Inner Circle countries. A major difference, however, is that whereas bilingual users in the Inner Circle countries may want to link their English learning and use with the culture of the country in which they live, bilingual users in other countries do not have this goal. This is a difference that will be fully examined when we discuss the link between culture and language learning in subsequent chapters.

Bilingual users of English in Expanding Circle countries

For bilingual users in Expanding Circle countries, English is used primarily as a language of wider communication across national and cultural boundaries. Hence, a Japanese businessperson might use English with a Brazilian businessperson in negotiating transactions, or a Chinese tourist might use English when traveling to Thailand. In such cases, English is used as the default language since no other alternative exists. The following example, in which the speakers are a Dane (H) and a Syrian (B), illustrates this use of English.

Example 2
> **B** So I told him not to send the cheese after the blowing in the customs. We don't want the order after the cheese is blowing.
> **H** I see, yes.
> **B** So I don't know what we can do with the order now. What do you think we should do with this all blowing, Mr. Hansen?

H I'm not uh (pause). Blowing? What is this, too big or what?
B No, the cheese is bad Mr. Hansen. It is like fermenting in the customs' cool rooms.
H Ah, it's gone off!
B Yes, it's gone off.
(Firth 1996, cited in Graddol 1997: 13).

This example illustrates what is often referred to as using English for international purposes, that is, the use of English as the default language for purposes of wider communication. In such contexts, the speakers have no other code available. There is, however, great variation in the use of English among countries of the Expanding Circle. As was pointed out in Chapter 1, in some countries like Denmark, Norway, and Sweden the use of the language within the country is so prevalent that they might be considered Outer Circle countries.

Redefining English as an international language

In examining the use of English as an international language, an important question is whether or not the use of English within multilingual countries like South Africa and Kenya is an example of the use of English as an international language. I would argue that in some sense it is. If one assumes that one of the essential characteristics of English as an international language is that English is used to communicate across linguistic and cultural boundaries, often in more formal contexts, then there seems little reason to require that these boundaries must coincide with national borders. Rather one could argue that whenever English is being used alongside other languages in a multilingual context as the unmarked choice for purposes of wider communication, English in some sense is being used as an international language. The difference is that when English is being used across borders, it is a global language of wider communication whereas when it is used within a country, it is a local language of wider communication.

Although some differentiate the use of English within national boundaries as English for intranational as opposed to international purposes, I maintain that the defining characteristic of an international language rests on its use as the unmarked choice for purposes of wider communication across linguistic and cultural boundaries regardless of whether or not these differences exist within or between national boundaries. Indeed one of the major impetuses for the macroacquisition of English has been the usefulness of English to provide a relatively neutral basis for communication between linguistic and cultural groups within nation states.

English fits into bilingual users' personal language hierarchies differently in different countries and in particular speech communities within those countries. In many cases their needs do not entail achieving native-like competence in English, yet most current SLA research rests on this assumption. We turn now to the problems of using a native speaker model in undertaking research regarding the current state of bilingual users of EIL. This is followed by a discussion of the kind of research that is presently needed to more fully understand what it means to acquire and use EIL in Outer and Expanding Circle countries.

Problems of using a native speaker model in research

It has generally been assumed that the ultimate goal of English language learners is to achieve native-like competence. Stern (1983), for example, maintains that 'the native speaker's "competence", "proficiency" or "knowledge of the language" is a necessary point of reference for the second language proficiency concept used in English teaching theory' (p. 341). Yet as more and more users of English come to use the language alongside one or more others, their use will be significantly different from that of monolingual speakers. Because bilingual speakers of English have different needs in using the language than do monolingual speakers, any comparison is unwarranted. However, as Cook (1999) notes,

> SLA research has often fallen into the *comparative fallacy* (Bley-Vroman 1983) of relating the L2 learner to the native speaker. This tendency is reflected in the frequency with which the words *succeed* and *fail* are associated with the phrase *native speaker*, for example, the view that fossilisation and errors in L2 users' speech add up to 'failure to achieve native-speaker competence'.
> (Cook 1999: 189)

Sridhar and Sridhar (1994) provide an excellent critique of traditional SLA research assumptions in regard to bilingual users of English outside Inner Circle countries. They contend that much SLA theory is not relevant to an investigation of these speakers because it often rests on assumptions that were developed and tested primarily in reference to the learning of English and European languages in the United States, with little input from the learning of English in other countries. The first assumption is that the learner's target is native-like competence. However, as Sridhar and Sridhar point out, many studies of what they term 'indigenized varieties of English or IVES' (e.g. Indian English, Nigerian English, Singaporean English) clearly demonstrate that a variety of English that is too closely aligned with an Inner Circle standard can be seen by speakers in the local speech

speech community to be 'distasteful and pedantic' and 'affected or even snobbish' (1994: 45). For this reason many learners of English do not want and may even reject a native-like target.

A second assumption that underlies much SLA research is that the input learners have available is extensive and intensive enough for them to acquire native-like competence. Yet for many English language learners in the Outer and Expanding Circle the nature of the input they receive is restricted in amount and quality. Often the learner is not exposed to the full range of styles, structures, and speech acts that supposedly is necessary to acquire native-like proficiency, whatever that may be; instead 'he or she gets exposed to a subset of registers, styles, speech event types—mainly academic, bureaucratic, and literary' (ibid.: 46–7).

The third problem that Sridhar and Sridhar contend exists in much SLA research is that the process of acquisition is not studied in reference to the functions that English serves within the local community. As we have just discussed, many bilingual users of English in Outer Circle countries use the language alongside others they speak, drawing on their rich linguistic repertoire to signal particular role relationships. In some cases English serves primarily as a formal register with respect to the other languages of the speech community. Hence, English does not serve all the functions it might for learners in the Inner Circle, who, in many cases, learn it as a replacement for their first language.

Another problem with much of the existing SLA research in reference to contributing to a better understanding of the use of English today in Outer and Expanding Circle countries is that the role of the learner's first language is considered in terms of how it interferes with or, in a few cases, how it facilitates the acquisition of English rather than considering how English contributes to an overall communication pattern in a multilingual setting. In addition, much SLA research assumes that the ideal motivation for learning English is integrative, which, in Sridhar and Sridhar's view, entails 'admiration for the native speakers of the target language and a desire to become a member of their culture' (1994: 44). However, in many countries, the acquisition of English is driven by what is typically called instrumental motivation, namely the desire to pass an English examination, to read books in English, or to access information on the Internet.

Sridhar and Sridhar argue that the lack of applicability of many assumptions underlying current SLA research is particularly disturbing in light of the fact that English learners outside of the Inner Circle 'numerically as well as in terms of the range and diversity of variables they represent, constitute one of the most significant segments of second language acquirers in the world today' (ibid.: 42). This segment is growing in size, and the varied uses of English among bilingual speakers in multilingual contexts warrants a good deal more research.

To undertake such research productively, the prevalent assumption in much SLA research that the goal of English language learning is to achieve native-like competence in the language must be put aside. It is important to do so for two reasons. First, if, as we demonstrated at the beginning of the chapter, the whole notion of defining a native speaker and native speaker competence is fraught with difficulty, it is unreasonable to take such a poorly defined construct as the basis for research into bilingual English language use. Second, an approach to SLA research that is based on the notion that all learners of English need or desire so-called 'native speaker competence' will contribute little to a better understanding of their various language needs.

As was argued earlier, EIL can be used as a language of wider com-munication within as well as across national borders, and research is needed into the functions that English serves within particular Outer Circle countries. How does English fit into the linguistic repertoire of bilingual users in these countries? In what contexts does the language serve as the unmarked code? How is the use of English within these countries related to educational level, economic status, and ethnic background? In addition, more research is needed on exactly how English is used as a language of wider communication between individuals from Outer and Expanding Circle countries. What strategies do such individuals use in repairing problems in comprehension? What does the use of English in such contexts suggest for linguistic standards and pronunciation models?

Clearly, teaching English as an international language requires that researchers and educators thoroughly examine individual learners' specific uses of English within their particular speech community as a basis for determining learning goals. Even more importantly it requires that they set aside the fallacy whereby multilingual speakers of English, both in research and pedagogy, are constantly compared with native speaker models. The comparison of bilingual users of English with native speaker models also needs to be challenged in reference to language teachers. To demonstrate the serious repercussions of applying native speaker models to language teachers, we turn now to an examination of bilingual teachers of English.

Bilingual teachers of English

Today 80 per cent of English language teaching professionals worldwide are bilingual users of English (Canagarajah 1999a). Despite this, the fallacy of comparing non-native English-speaking teaching professionals to native speakers is widespread. Just as it is unreasonable to take the poorly defined construct of native speaker as the basis for SLA research, it is unwarranted to take this construct as the basis for judging pedagogic expertise. As Canagarajah points out, the acceptance of the native speaker fallacy is both linguistically inaccurate and politically damaging. The native speaker fallacy is based on the Chomskyan notion that the native speaker is the ideal informant in grammatical judgments and is therefore the ultimate authority on language use. Yet such a notion is 'linguistically anachronistic' since it 'flies in the face of some basic linguistic concepts developed through research and accepted by contemporary scholars' (1999a: 79). Most linguists agree that all languages and dialects are of equal status, that languages in contact always undergo change, and that variants of a language are appropriate in particular contexts.

One of the most unfortunate repercussions of the acceptance of the native speaker fallacy in reference to language teaching is its positioning of bilingual users of English in the ELT job market. Invariably in hiring practices, it is the native speaker that is given preference. Govardhan, Nayar, and Sheorey (1999), for example, found that in their survey of advertisements for teaching English abroad, the main and perhaps only common requirement was being a native or native-like speaker of English. Many private language institutes find that they can charge more if they advertise they have native English speakers as teachers. Hence, in many English teaching institutions around the world, the (so-called) native speaker of English is given preference in hiring. Such a perspective places the bilingual teacher of English at a severe disadvantage in the job market. Liu (1999), for example, in his research on bilingual professionals in TESOL notes that all of the people he interviewed had experienced discrimination in hiring practices.

An acceptance of the native speaker fallacy in reference to language teaching also frequently reinforces a narrow definition of pedagogical expertise, one in which a great deal of prestige is given to native-like pronunciation and intuition. As Canagarajah (1999a) notes, this narrow view of professionalism can have damaging effects on bilingual English teachers in the Outer and Expanding Circle:

> Many Periphery professionals feel compelled to spend undue time repairing their pronunciation or performing other cosmetic changes to sound native. Their predominant concern is in effect 'How can I lose my accent?' rather than 'How can I be a successful teacher?' The anxiety and inhibitions about their pronunciation can make them lose their grip on the instructional process or lack rapport with their students.
> (Canagarajah 1999a: 84–5)

In reference to pronunciation, once again the native speaker model needs to be carefully examined. As Jenkins (1998) points out, a more realistic approach to pronunciation may be to treat the native speaker model not as a goal for production but rather as a point of reference to prevent non-native varieties from moving too far apart from each other. This important question of pronunciation models and norms will be fully examined in the next chapter.

However, pronunciation is not the only factor that can lead bilingual English teachers to experience a good deal of insecurity in their own abilities. Tang (1997), for example, reports on a survey she conducted of a teacher retraining course in Hong Kong in which she asked local teachers about their perceptions of the proficiency of native- and non-native-speaking teachers of English. A very high percentage of the teachers believed that native English-speaking teachers were superior to non-native English-speaking teachers in speaking (100 per cent), pronunciation (92 per cent), listening (87 per cent), vocabulary (79 per cent), and reading (72 per cent). Seidlhofer (1999), in her survey of English teachers in Austria, found that a majority (57 per cent) of the respondents stated that being a non-native speaker of English made them feel insecure.

The insecurity of bilingual English teachers is perhaps even more acutely felt when these teachers are working in Inner Circle countries. Thomas (1999), for example, whose first language is Indian/Singapore English, recounts her experiences in teaching in an intensive English program in the United States. She describes how, on various occasions, students re-ported how disappointed they were when they first saw her, a 'foreigner' with a different accent. Some added that they had paid a good deal of money to come to the United States and that they were hoping to get a native speaker as a teacher. For Thomas, such experiences made her question her credibility and ability, leading to a kind of paranoia. My research on Japanese graduate students completing their practicum in the United States further demonstrates the insecurity that can be felt by bilingual ELT professionals in Inner Circle countries (McKay 2000b). Not only did these teachers feel insecure in terms of pronunciation and linguistic knowledge, but they also felt inadequate in terms of their cultural knowledge regarding the United States. The fact that in their eyes they were less competent teachers of English because they did not have specific knowledge about cultural aspects of the United States suggests that they viewed the acquisition of English as necessarily linked to acquiring the culture and identity of an Inner Circle country. Yet, as was pointed out in Chapter 1, an international language is by definition a language that belongs to all those who speak it and not to the few who acquire and use it from childhood.

But why this shows went to the acquni tttem with fw

It is encouraging, however, that more and more educators today are challenging the native speaker fallacy and pointing out the many strengths of competent teachers of English who share a first language with their students and have gone through the process of learning English as an additional language. Medgyes, for example, while arguing that bilingual users of English can never achieve native-like competence, nonetheless maintains that bilingual teachers (what he terms non-native English-speaking teachers or non-NESTs) have the following advantages as teachers.

 a Only non-NESTs can serve as imitable models of the successful learner of English . . .
 b Non-NESTs can teach learning strategies more effectively . . .
 c Non-NESTs can provide learners with more information about the English language . . .
 d Non-NESTs are more able to anticipate language difficulties . . .
 e Non-NESTs can be more empathetic to the needs and problems of their learners . . .
 f Only non-NESTs can benefit from sharing the learners' mother tongue . . .
 (Medgyes 1992: 346–7)

Although it is encouraging that Medgyes emphasizes the strengths of bilingual teachers of English, his discussion is highly problematic in that it too rests on an acceptance of the native speaker fallacy in which bilingual teachers are compared with so-called native speakers. Such an approach is not productive in examining the benefits of bilingualism and biculturalism in the teaching of EIL. Bilingual teachers in Outer Circle countries, for example, are aware of how English fits into the linguistic repertoire of their students. They are familiar with the different varieties of English spoken within the country and where these varieties are appropriately used. They also possess an understanding of the local culture, knowledge that is crucial in the teaching of EIL, where, as was pointed out in Chapter 1, the purpose of acquiring the language is to communicate local cultural knowledge to others. Only when the native speaker fallacy is put aside can a full exploration of such strengths of bilingual teachers be undertaken.

Seidlhofer (1999) has contributed to this process by describing the many strengths of bilingual teachers of English. As she points out, bilingual ELT professionals teaching in their own country are in a sense 'double agents' in that they know the language and culture of their students as well as the target language. This makes them 'uniquely suited to be agents facilitating learning by mediating between the different languages and cultures through appropriate pedagogy' (p. 235). The ability of local teachers to design appropriate pedagogy should not be underestimated since they are in the best position to be able to assess the effectiveness of methods and materials for their local context. This is an issue we will return to in the final two chapters of the book.

Another advantage of bilingual English teachers is that, since they have gone through the process of acquiring English as a second language themselves, they often have a highly developed awareness of the structure of the language; in addition, they can anticipate the problems their students may have in acquiring it. As Seidlhofer (1999) notes, this ability enables bilingual teachers to 'get into the skin of the foreigner learner' (p. 243). Ultimately, being able to do this provides bilingual teachers with a keen sense of what their students need to know. But perhaps the greatest strength of bilingual English teachers is that they provide their students with a model of a good language learner that is relevant to their own social and cultural experiences, a model that no language teacher from another culture can ever provide.

If English continues to spread, it is clear that the majority of users in the coming decades will be bilinguals who use the language, alongside one or more others, largely for purposes of wider communication. As this chapter has argued, in meeting the pedagogical needs of such users it is essential that the native speaker fallacy be challenged. Challenging this fallacy will hopefully lead to a more complete picture of how English is used in many communities around the world, a better understanding of how it is acquired in various contexts, and a more accurate interpretation of the strengths of bilingual English-speaking professionals.

Summary

This chapter has explored the various ways in which bilingual users of English make use of the language for purposes of wider communication. Central to it has been the notion that bilingual users vary widely in the manner in which they do this, some using English within a rich linguistic repertoire that consists of several languages. Because of the great diversity of bilingual users of English, comparing them to native speakers, for both pedagogical and research purposes, is unproductive. Furthermore, such an approach assumes that what constitutes a native speaker is clear, an assumption that is completely unwarranted in light of the controversy surrounding attempts to define the term.

The chapter has emphasized that, in general, the needs of bilingual users in Inner Circle countries and Outer or Expanding Circle countries are quite different, with the former learning English because of migration and often having the intent to acculturate to a new environment. However, it was also noted that in some instances this distinction is inadequate since some bilinguals in the Outer Circle have come to use English in ways very similar to many Inner Circle users. Given the growing number of bilingual users of English and the great diversity that exists among them, it is essential that more research be undertaken on the various ways these individuals make use of English. To be most productive, such research should not be based on a native speaker model, a model that has informed a good deal of existing SLA research.

The chapter concluded with an examination of the negative effects of applying the native speaker fallacy to bilingual teachers of English, pointing out the many strengths of bilingual teachers who share their students' culture. We turn now to a discussion of language standards in reference to EIL. We will examine the question of standards on various levels—grammatical, lexical, phonological, pragmatic and discourse—and relate the discussion to the notion of language change and the ownership of an international language.

Further reading

On the term native speaker and the native speaker fallacy

Cook, V. 1999. 'Going beyond the native speaker in language teaching.' *TESOL Quarterly* 33: 185–209.

Davies, A. 1991. *The Native Speaker in Applied Linguistics*. Edinburgh: Edinburgh University Press.

Rampton, M. B. H. 1990. 'Displacing the native speaker: expertise, affiliation, and inheritance.' *ELT Journal* 44: 97–101.

Sridhar, S. N. and K. K. Sridhar. 1994. 'Indigenized Englishes as second languages: toward a functional theory of second language acquisition in multilingual contexts' in Agnihotri, R. K. and A. L. Khanna (eds): *Second Language Acquisition: Socio-Cultural and Linguistic Aspects of English in India*. London: Sage Publications: 41–63.

On codeswitching in multilingual societies

Myers-Scotton, C. 1993. *Social Motivations for Codeswitching*. Oxford: Clarendon Press.

Sridhar, K. K. 1996. 'Societal multilingualism' in McKay, S. L. and N. H. Hornberger (eds): *Sociolinguistics and Language Teaching*. Cambridge: Cambridge University Press: 47–71.

On bilingual teachers of English

Braine, G. (ed.) 1999. *Non-Native Educators in English Language Teaching.* Mahwah, NJ: Lawrence Erlbaum Associates.

Medgyes, P. 1992. 'Native or non-native: Who's worth more?' *ELT Journal* 46/4: 340–9.

Medgyes, P. 1994. *The Non-Native Teacher.* Hong Kong: Macmillan Publishers, Inc.

3 STANDARDS FOR ENGLISH AS AN INTERNATIONAL LANGUAGE

Why is the issue of standards of primary concern in the study of EIL? As this chapter demonstrates, in many Outer Circle countries, bilingual speakers of English are using the language on a daily basis alongside one or more others and frequently their use of English is influenced by these other languages. Hence, they are developing new lexical items, new grammatical standards, and their pronunciation is also being influenced by their other languages. These changes lead some people to worry that English will vary to such an extent that it will no longer serve the main purpose of an international language, namely to provide a link across cultures and languages. Thus, it is critical that we examine what is meant by standards, what mutual *intelligibility* involves, and what changes have occurred in different varieties of English.

The chapter begins by discussing the notion of standards and explaining what factors are needed to determine whether or not an innovation has been accepted as a standard. It emphasizes how language spread necessarily involves language change and examines various attitudes that exist among bilingual users of English to their variety of English, as well as to *Standard English*. The chapter then describes and exemplifies present-day variation in English on a lexical, grammatical, and phonological level, stressing that the extent of variation on these levels can vary greatly within a country. It ends with an examination of how the native speaker model has been applied to L2 pedagogy and research in regard to pragmatic and textual competence, and argues for the need to recognize a variety of pragmatic and textual norms in the use of EIL.

Language standards and English as an international language

The issue of standards exists in all languages. The Académie française, for example, is charged with the responsibility of upholding particular standards in the use of French. Whereas no comparable body exists to regulate the use of English, the desire to uphold standards is clearly present. With the spread of English and the resulting variation in the language, some people believe that the need to uphold common standards has increased in importance. It is puzzling that whereas differences in the use of English between Inner Circle countries are generally accepted, with no one suggesting that this will lead to incomprehensibility, language variation outside Inner Circle countries is often seen as a threat. Brutt-Griffler (1998) argues that such tolerance must be extended:

> Most, if not all, Inner Circle English speakers appear willing to meet on a common linguistic plane, accept the diversity of their Englishes, and do not require of one another to prove competence in English, despite the considerable differences in the varieties of English they speak and the cross-communication problems entailed thereby . . . this situation must be extended to all English-using communities. (Brutt-Griffler 1998: 389)

At present, however, such tolerance is not extended to innovations that occur outside Inner Circle countries; rather, many linguists argue that one variety of English must be promoted and a concerted effort made to teach standards.

The debate over standards in English as an international language

The debate over standards was a major topic at a 1984 conference to celebrate the fiftieth anniversary of the British Council. (See Quirk and Widdowson (1985) for papers delivered at this conference.) At this conference, Randolph Quirk and Braj Kachru, two key figures in the debate over standards in EIL, expressed very different views on the issue. Quirk argued for the need to uphold standards in the use of English in both Inner Circle countries and those outside the Inner Circle. He maintained that tolerance for variation in language use was educationally damaging in Inner Circle countries and that 'the relatively narrow range of purposes for which the non-native needs to use English . . . is arguably well catered for by a single monochrome standard form that looks as good on paper as it sounds in speech' (Quirk 1985: 6). In other words, for Quirk, a common standard of use is warranted in all contexts of English language use.

Kachru (1985), on the other hand, argued that the spread of English had brought with it a need to re-examine traditional notions of standardization and models as they relate to Outer Circle users. As he put it,

In my view, the global diffusion of English has taken an interesting turn: the native speakers of this language seem to have lost the exclusive prerogative to control its standardization; in fact, if current statistics are any indication, they have become a minority. This sociolinguistic fact must be accepted and its implication recognized. What we need now are new paradigms and perspectives for linguistic and pedagogical research and for understanding the linguistic creativity in multilingual situations across cultures.
(Kachru 1985: 30)

Kachru argued for a recognition of norms based on the manner in which English is used within particular speech communities, both native-speaking communities and those in the Outer Circle. He maintained that allowing for a variety of norms would not lead to a lack of intelligibility among varieties of English; rather, what would emerge from this situation would be an educated variety that would be intelligible across the others.

Defining Standard English

Central to this debate, of course, is what is meant by standards or norms. In his discussion of *Standard English*, Strevens (1983) defines Standard English as

A particular dialect of English, being the only non-localized dialect, of global currency without significant variation, universally accepted as the appropriate educational target in teaching English; which may be spoken with an unrestricted choice of accent.
(Strevens 1983: 88)

What is significant in this definition is that for Strevens there is no standardized accent associated with Standard English. This will be important when we consider the issue of phonological variation in EIL. Others associate Standard English particularly with the written form of language. Quirk (1990), for example, maintains that Standard English is what might be termed the unmarked variety; it is not unusual or different in any way and is typically associated with written English.

The *Longman Dictionary of Applied Linguistics* (Richards, Platt, and Weber 1985) also associates Standard English with written language and it notes its status in relation to other varieties. It defines Standard English as

the variety of a language which has the highest status in a community or nation and which is usually based on the speech and writing of educated speakers of the language.
A standard variety is generally:
(a) used in the news media and in literature

(b) described in dictionaries and grammars
(c) taught in schools and taught to non-native speakers when they learn the language as a foreign language.
(ibid.: 271)

When changes occur in an Outer Circle country and when such innovations get conventionally established by regular use, some argue that they should be considered as standard for that particular context. The problem, however, is determining exactly when an innovation can be considered a standard or norm. Bamgbose (1998) delineates five factors that can be used to determine whether or not an innovation is a norm. They are

• demographic (How many people use the innovation?)
• geographical (How widely is the innovation used within the country?)
• authoritative (Who uses the innovation?)
• codification (Where is the usage sanctioned?)
• acceptability (What is the attitude of users and non-users toward the innovation?).

Bamgbose contends that the most important factors in determining if an innovation can be considered a norm is whether or not the innovation is *codified* in such things as dictionaries, coursebooks, or other manuals, and whether or not it is widely accepted.

The question of intelligibility

If different norms develop in different varieties of EIL, will this ultimately lead to a lack of mutual intelligibility among them? To answer this question we need to consider what is meant by *intelligibility*. This is a complex matter, involving what some linguists refer to as 'intelligibility' (recognizing an expression), *comprehensibility* (knowing the meaning of the expression), and *interpretability* (knowing what the expression signifies in a particular sociocultural context). For example, if a listener recognizes that the word *salt* is an English word rather than a Spanish word, English is then intelligible to him or her. If the listener in addition knows the meaning of the word, it is comprehensible, and if he or she understands that the phrase 'Do you have any salt?' is intended to be a request for salt, then he or she is said to be able to interpret the language.

Whereas these are important distinctions to make in discussing the issue of intelligibility, often the term is used to cover all three types of meaning given above, and for the most part we will use the word in this more general sense in the discussion that follows. Meanwhile, it is worth noting that in many ways it is what is referred to as interpretability that causes the greatest problems in the use of EIL for cross-cultural communication since interpretability entails questions of culture and context. This is because the listener must be able to understand a speaker's intentions even when they are expressed indirectly as in the example above, 'Do you have any salt?' However, it is important to note that when English is used cross culturally, it is very possible that the speakers will work together to achieve interpretability. Bamgboṣe (1998) emphasizes this fact when he notes, 'Preoccupation with intelligibility has often taken an abstract form characterized by decontextualized comparison of varieties. The point is often missed that it is people, not language codes, that understand one another' (p. 11). Clearly a willingness to be involved in matters of interpretation needs to exist if communication is to take place between speakers of different varieties of EIL, an issue we will return to later in the chapter.

Given the spread of English there is no question that many varieties will develop, each with its own norms. Yet the fact that many bilingual users of English acquire the language in an educational context in which particular standards of use are emphasized will likely ensure some unifying norms. Indeed, unifying norms are needed if English is to serve purposes of wider communication. As Widdowson (1994) notes,

> As soon as you accept that English serves the communicative and communal needs of different communities, it follows logically that it must be diverse. An international language has to be an independent language. It does not follow logically, however, that the language will disperse into mutually unintelligible varieties. For it will naturally stabilize into standard form to the extent required to meet the needs of the communities concerned. Thus it is clearly vital to the interests of the international community . . . that they should preserve a common standard of English in order to keep up standards of communicative effectiveness.
> (Widdowson 1994: 385)

Language change and varieties of English

As was noted in Chapter 1, the early spread of English was fueled primarily by speaker migration from the United Kingdom, resulting in the development of Inner Circle varieties of English. The language change that occurred in these countries has been largely codified and widely accepted. The current spread of EIL has occurred primarily through the macro-acquisition of English by existing speech communities, resulting in a tremendous growth in the number of bilingual users of English. It is within the so-called Outer Circle countries, in which English has some type of official status within the country, that the greatest controversy regarding language change and questions of intelligibility has arisen.

Kachru (1986) refers to the varieties of English used in many Outer Circles countries as institutionalized or nativized . He contends that, because in these countries English serves a wide range of functions in the local educational, administrative, and legal systems, the use of the language has become institutionalized, resulting in the development of new norms which have become codified and accepted. As pointed out earlier, at the 1984 conference Kachru argued for a recognition of norms based on the manner in which English is used within particular speech communities. He argued that whereas Inner Circle countries are usually considered to be *norm-providing speech communities*, Outer Circle countries are *norm-developing* communities since innovations in these countries get conventionally established by regular use and are subsequently codified. He also suggested that in the Expanding Circle, where English does not have an official role, its use should be *norm-dependent* since there is no regular internal use of the language. In this respect, Kachru and Quirk are in agreement.

Whereas many Outer Circle countries have developed new standards of use, each country in the Outer Circle exemplifies a distinct historical, acquisitional, and cultural context in reference to the spread of English. Hence, the use of English in each of these countries is unique in the extent of change that has occurred and the manner in which the local community has accepted these changes. In order to demonstrate the unique development of English within specific contexts, we now turn to a comparison of the use of English and the attitudes toward change that exist within two Outer Circle countries, India and Singapore. These countries were selected because in general applied linguists and educators based in them exemplify contrasting attitudes toward their own *nativized variety* of English (or *World English*).

Attitudes toward varieties of English

In analyzing the varieties of English spoken in Singapore, Lick and Alsagoff (1998) point out that varieties of any language are associated with particular social groups and can be characterized by a specific set of linguistic variations. In addition, they note that from a linguist's point of view, all varieties of English are equal because they are fully systematic and regulated by a set of rules. They give an example of a sentence from what is termed 'Singlish', a particular variety of English spoken in informal contexts in Singapore. The sentence 'She kena sabo by them' is equivalent to the Standard English sentence 'She was sabotaged by them'. Lick and Alsagoff point out that this Singlish sentence is grammatical in that the sentence conforms to the grammatical rules of Singlish. Put another way, if these words were arranged in any other order, they would not be considered grammatical by speakers of Singlish. Thus, Singlish is a valid grammatical variety of English, linguistically equal to any other variety of English. When, however, Singlish was used on a local Singaporean television entertainment program, it led to tremendous controversy, with some Singaporeans urging the authorities to step in and regulate the use of Singlish on television so that children would not speak what they termed 'bad English'. Others, however, defended the use of Singlish, claiming that this variety of English was part of the Singaporean identity and that ordinary people could relate to it.

A controversy such as this highlights the fact that whereas all varieties of English are linguistically equal, they are not considered to be socially equal. The variety with the most prestige is typically referred to as Standard English, with all other varieties generally labeled with pejorative terms such as sub-standard or non-standard. As Lick and Alsagoff note,

> Generally, the variety spoken by the socially dominant group, which normally includes the rich and powerful, as well as the educated elite, has the most prestige. This variety is then institutionalized as the standard: it is used for governmental administration and on all formal occasions. It is taught in schools and used in the mass media (on television, radio, and in the press) and it serves as the model for those who wish to master the language. In contrast, the varieties used by people of lower social status, such as the poor and the uneducated, are tagged as *nonstandard*, sometimes derogatorily as *substandard* synonymous with words such as *bad, corrupt,* and *offensive*. Such a standard–nonstandard division is basically a reflection of social inequality.
> (Lick and Alsagoff 1998: 282)

Whereas Lick and Alsagoff's description of standard and non-standard English is significant in its recognition of the prevalent association of Standard English with social class and status, it does not elaborate on the various ways in which specific varieties of English can be used within a country. In the case of Singlish, in some instances, the non-standard variety is in fact used by speakers of the socially dominant group as well as speakers of lower social status, but the former generally only use it in informal contexts to signal social identity and rapport. However, Singlish is the only variety many less powerful, less educated Singaporeans have available to them and is therefore often considered to be non-standard or sub-standard. In many countries where an institutionalized variety of English exists there is a dual attitude toward the use of some local indigenized varieties like Singlish. Although for some the local variety represents a means for speakers to take ownership of the language and thus express their own identity, for others the indigenized variety represents a corruption or sub-standard use.

Kachru (1986) notes that the varieties of English that exist within Outer Circle countries often represent a cline, with some varieties like Singlish serving more local or national purposes, whereas what is termed Standard English reaches a more extensive audience. He uses the term *cline of bilingualism* to describe the range of varieties of English used by individuals within one country. Hence, one can speak of an individual's cline of bilingualism ranging from the variety he or she typically uses in the local market to the variety he or she generally uses in educational or business contexts. In some cases, however, as we have seen, an individual may not have access to all the varieties of English spoken in the country. This cline can be represented by an English language hierarchy for Singapore shown in Figure 3.1 that is similar to the personal language hierarchy shown in Chapter 2 in Figure 2.3. The inverted pyramid illustrates that Standard English has a greater territorial reach. However, the other varieties of English are important elements of an individual's linguistic repertoire, allowing levels of formality and role relationships to be signaled.

In many ways, in their rhetoric and policies, Singaporeans and Indians have very different attitudes regarding the value of their local indigenized variety of English. This difference is evident in the findings of an early study of language attitudes and indigenized varieties of English in the two countries (Shaw 1983). Shaw asked college students from both countries what variety of English they believed should be learned—British English, American English, Australian English or the nativized variety. Whereas a large number of Indians were in favor of promoting their own variety of English, Singaporeans were equally divided between accepting a British

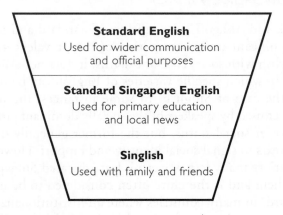

Figure 3.1: English language hierarchy for Singapore

standard and their own nativized variety. This general pattern of opinion in the two countries is evident even today.

Pakir (1998), for example, points out that whereas local varieties of English in Singapore are often used to express the cultural and national identities of its inhabitants, Singapore, as a small young country, 'needs and uses English for international purposes, and does so at a level that is perhaps unprecedented in comparison to other countries in the Outer Circle' (p. 82). It is Singapore's focus on the value of English for wider communication for economic purposes that has perhaps fueled a belief among educational leaders in Singapore that the schools must actively promote the acquisition of a standard variety of English for all Singaporeans. This has led to a massive project to promote grammatical correctness in the state schools.

In India, on the other hand, there is widespread support for the promotion of local varieties of English, as is evident in many of the works of well-known Indian English writers. Raja Rao (1978), for example, writes

> And as long as the English language is universal, it will always remain Indian . . . It would then be correct to say as long as we are Indian—that is, not nationalists, but truly Indians of the Indian psyche—we shall have the English language with us and amongst us, and not as a guest or friend, but as one of our own, of our caste, our creed, our sect and of our tradition.
> (Rao 1978, as cited in Kachru 1996: 25)

And Anita Desai states

> If a writer is Indian . . . his work will naturally be Indian in quality, in flavour, in its characteristics . . . it can hardly be anything else, even if he is writing in English. The English spoken and written in India has in any case become an Indian language.
> (interview with Anita Desai, quoted by Ram 1983: 32–3)

What do such varying attitudes toward nativized varieties of English suggest for the teaching of EIL? First, they demonstrate that many bilingual speakers of English, both as individuals and as teachers and educational leaders, will have mixed attitudes toward their use of the language. Whereas in many cases they have taken ownership of English and changed the language, they themselves will be measuring their use of English against what they perceive as the standard or correct variety, approaching the use of English not in any purely linguistic sense, but rather in its social context of prestige and power. Second, the cline of English spoken within many Outer Circle countries highlights an important strength of bilingual teachers of English. It is these teachers, not native speakers of English, who will best know how to use the varieties of English spoken in the country appropriately. Gupta (1998), for example, points out how valuable she believes the use of Singapore colloquial English can be in the primary years in helping children acquire Singapore Standard English.

Distinctive linguistic features of varieties of English

As was pointed out above, the English spoken in various Outer Circle countries typically consists of a cline ranging from a standard variety to one that is unique to the area. Tay (1982), for example, describes the cline in Singapore as consisting of a *basilect, mesolect,* and *acrolect.* These terms were first used by Bickerton (1975) to describe variation within creoles and have subsequently been used to describe language variation in other contexts. For Bickerton, an acrolect refers to the variety of a creole that has no significant difference from Standard English, often spoken by the most educated speakers; the mesolect has unique grammatical features that distinguish it from Standard English; and the basilect, often spoken by the less educated people of the society, has very significant grammatical difference.

In reference to Singapore, Tay points out that the acrolect has no significant grammatical differences from Standard British English and typically differs in vocabulary only by extending the meaning of existing words, for example, using the word 'bungalow' to refer to a two-storied building. The mesolect, on the other hand, has a number of unique grammatical features such as the dropping of some indefinite articles and the lack of plural marking on some count nouns. Also there are several loan words from Chinese and Malay. The basilect has more significant grammatical differences such as copula deletion and *do*-deletion in direct questions. It is also characterized by the use of words that are typically considered slang or colloquialisms.

Bamgboṣe (1992) notes that there have been different ways of characteriz-ing the varieties of English spoken in Nigeria. In some descriptions, these varieties are linked to the level of education that an individual has attained, ranging from a pidgin variety spoken by those with no formal education to a Standard English variety spoken by those with a university education. The correlation between level of education and variety of English spoken in Nigeria supports the contention discussed earlier that level of education, often related to economic class, plays a key role in the spread of English and in an individual's access to the prestige forms of English.

He cites others, like Banjo, who distinguish varieties on the basis of specific linguistic characteristics, international intelligibility, and social acceptability. In the following description Variety 1 might be considered a basilect, Variety 2 a mesolect, and Varieties 3 and 4 acrolects.

> *Variety 1:* Marked by wholesale transfer of phonological, syntactic, and lexical features of Kwa or Niger-Congo to English. Spoken by those whose knowledge of English is very imperfect. Neither socially acceptable in Nigeria nor internationally intelligible.
>
> *Variety 2:* Syntax close to that of Standard British English, but with strongly marked phonological and lexical peculiarities. Spoken by up to 75 per cent of those who speak English in the country. Socially acceptable, but with rather low international intelligibility.
>
> *Variety 3:* Close to Standard British English both in syntax and in semantics; similar in phonology, but different in phonetic features as well as with regard to certain lexical peculiarities. Socially acceptable and internationally intelligible. Spoken by less than 10 per cent of the population.
>
> *Variety 4:* Identical with Standard British English in syntax and semantics, having identical phonological and phonetic features of a British regional dialect of English. Maximally internationally in-telligible, but socially unacceptable. Spoken by only a handful of Nigerians born or brought up in England.
>
> (Banjo 1971, as cited in Bamgboṣe 1992: 149–50)

The significant feature of this description of Nigerian English is that it suggests that only a small percentage of Nigerians speak a variety of English that is internationally intelligible (Varieties 3 and 4). Furthermore, those who speak Variety 4 are not socially acceptable within Nigeria itself. In fact, some varieties of English have special terms for those who have been to England and have acquired British Received Pronunciation (BRP) such as 'been-to boys' (Ghana) and 'England-returned' (India).

Bamgboṣe (1992) also points out that linguists who attempt to explain the differences that exist in Nigerian varieties of English typically use one of three approaches: an interference approach, a deviation approach, or a creativity approach. In an interference approach, differences are attributed to the influence of Nigerian languages. For Bamgboṣe, while this approach makes the most sense in explaining the phonetics of Nigerian English, there are some typical features of the pronunciation of Nigerian speakers of English that could not be predicted on the basis of the mother tongue of the speaker. In the case of lexis and syntax he finds the idea of inter-ference even less acceptable since most features cut across all first-language backgrounds. The deviation approach compares all features of Nigerian English with the English spoken by native speakers and labels them as deviant on the basis of either interference or imperfect learning. As

Bamgboṣe points out, the problem with this approach is that it ignores the fact that some of these features are recognized and codified, serving as identifying markers of Nigerian speakers. The creativity approach focuses on the exploitation of the resources of Nigerian languages as well as English to create new expressions. As Bamgboṣe notes, the main advantage of this approach is that 'it recognizes the development of Nigerian English as a type of its own right' (1992: 153).

Several problems exist in characterizing the varieties of English spoken within Outer Circle countries. First of all, within these countries the varieties are not clearly demarcated. Second, it is difficult to ascertain whether a particular usage is due to interference, lack of linguistic knowledge, or creativity on the part of the speaker. Finally, many problems exist in determining whether or not a particular feature has become a norm. With these problems in mind, we now turn to a discussion of the types of lexical, syntactic, and phonological innovations that are occurring in many of the varieties of English spoken in the Outer Circle countries. In each case we will highlight the kinds of methods that are used to distinguish these features.

Lexical variation

Like all linguistic innovation, it is difficult to ascertain the status of a particular word—is it widely used, socially accepted, and agreed upon in meaning? As Butler (1999), editor of *The Macquarie Dictionary*, points out, the opinion of a native speaker regarding the acceptability of a particular lexical item is not sufficient because language is constantly changing and because 'even native speakers can be wrong, if that is defined as being out of step with the majority' (1999: 189). As a result, lexicographers have come to rely on corpus materials to verify their intuitions. The value of a corpus, however, greatly depends on what is selected for inclusion. In the case of *The Macquarie Dictionary*, the purpose was to compile a dictionary of English that included generally accepted lexical items that were unique to specific countries in south-east Asia. In order to do this, the editors gathered a written corpus from representative countries that included fiction, non-fiction, and newspapers in English. This was then checked against the words in an earlier edition of *The Macquarie Dictionary* that included essentially Australian English words. Words that did not exist in the earlier version were considered as possible items of a local variety of English.

According to Butler, vocabulary items that are representative of local varieties of English appear to fall into a number of categories. One category is words that describe the details of daily life like *dirty kitchen* (Philippine English) and *outstation* (Singaporean and Malaysian English). A second category includes words that describe housing like *shophouse* (Singaporean and Malaysian English) and *sala* (Philippine English). Food items (e.g. *moon cakes*, Singaporean and Malaysian English, and *lecon*, Philippine English) and societal institutions (e.g. *minor wife*, Thai English, and *clansman*, Hong Kong English) are other categories of words. Other items express national identity like *Asian values* (Singaporean and Malaysian English) and *sanuk* (Thai English). What the corpus provides are lexical items in context. For example, listed below are the contexts for some of the words cited above.

> *outstation* (Singapore and Malaysian English) Citation: *Stand Alone*, Simon Tay, 1990.
> 'Hullo, is the Head in?' 'He's outstation. Who's calling?' 'Ya, conference, in Hawaii. Who's calling?'
>
> *clansman* (Hong Kong English) Citation: *Insights Guide*: Hong Kong, 1992.
> Besides Chinese weddings are dear. Banquets for the entertaining of clansmen can cost up to tens of thousands of dollars . . .
>
> *minor wife* (Thai English) Citation: *Bight of Bangkok*, Michael Smithies, 1993.
> Montana asked no questions, and was given enough to keep her happy. She invested not only in chit funds but also, more sensibly, in jewels. She was not prepared to be an impoverished first wife if Saiyud took a mistress, or a minor wife in the local parlance.
>
> (Butler 1996: 352–3)

Whereas the meaning of some of the words is clear from the context provided (e.g. *minor wife*), for others (e.g. *outstation*) the context does not provide sufficient clues to make the meaning clear. Hence, for readers unfamiliar with these words, there is a potential problem of comprehensibility. Given this fact, one would imagine that those who argue that potentially innovations in varieties of English will lead to a loss of mutual intelligibility would focus particularly on lexical innovation. Yet this is not generally the case. Rather it is grammatical changes that cause the greatest concern. Shortly we will consider some of the reasons for this situation.

Although it is clear that lexical innovation is a vital part of the changes that are occurring in the development of EIL, attitudes toward these changes vary significantly. In many cases, these variations in attitude seem to reflect whether or not the bilingual English user is from an Outer Circle or Expanding Circle country. Butler (1999), for example, in her survey of Filipino and Thai attitudes toward lexical innovation, found that most of the Filipino participants believed that local lexical items should take their place in a dictionary of Asian English. The primary concern was which words to include in the dictionary. The Thai participants, on the other hand, were much less likely to want to include any local English words. A survey of Malaysian attitudes toward lexical innovation (Crismore, Ngeow, and Soo 1996) also revealed negative attitudes. In the case of Malaysia, the fact that English has a much more restricted official role than it once did may play a part in this. Hence, in general, it may be that in any given country, the more English is used on a daily basis in a multilingual context, the more likely individuals in that country are to accept lexical innovation. The coining of new words, however, is not the only type of innovation that is occurring in various varieties of English. Grammatical changes are also developing.

Grammatical variation

Those who investigate grammatical variation in English typically begin by examining a written corpus of a particular variety in order to ascertain usages that are not typical of standard varieties. They then proceed to determine the acceptability of the usage by both native speakers and speakers of the variety in question. A summary of the findings of some representative studies of grammatical variation will demonstrate typical methods used and the types of variation that are occurring in new varieties of English.

Shastri (1996), for example, compared examples of complementation in three comparable corpora—an American corpus, a British corpus, and an Indian corpus. Each corpus consisted of 500 texts of approximately 2,000 words drawn from a variety of genres. Shastri was investigating the claim that complementation in Indian English frequently does not conform to Standard English usage, resulting in sentences like: 'External courses are meant for those persons who are interested *to enrich their knowledge*', and 'But when they wanted to celebrate Quarbana in the morning they prevented him *to do so*'. Shastri focused on a comparison of 29 specific examples of complementation among the three corpora. He found that the majority of complementation in the Indian corpus did conform to standard usage, and even in the cases where sentences displayed deviant uses, very few of these were statistically significant. Shastri concludes that if such examples of deviant use can also be found in a native variety corpus, then 'the burden of determining variety features shifts to quantitative studies, that is, research on the frequency of the so-called deviant features of a non-native variety of English compared to their frequencies in native varieties' (pp. 80–1). Shastri's findings challenge the contention that there is a deterioration of standards in new varieties of English. The fact that very few of the deviant uses were statistically significant demonstrates that, in general, written texts published in India exemplify the complementation patterns of Standard English.

Clearly the choice of corpora significantly affects findings relating to grammatical innovation. The Shastri study used corpora from published texts, which had probably been edited to conform to standard usage. Studies using unpublished written texts are likely to include more examples of non-standard usage. A study by Parasher (1994) is one such example. Parasher based his study on the grammatical, lexical, and stylistic features of Indian English contained in the correspondence (85 letters) of bank managers, administrative officials, scientists, and researchers working at a bank and a research institute in the Hyderabad area. Parasher asked two native speakers of British English, two of American English, and two university level Indian teachers of English to underline expressions they considered unacceptable.

Notice that the informants were asked to judge the acceptability of the items and not their intelligibility. Judgments of acceptability have to do with whether or not an item is considered correct and appropriate for a particular context. Whereas an item could be judged acceptable in one context (e.g. the use of a Singlish expression in an informal context in Singapore), it might be unintelligible to many speakers of English and inappropriate in other contexts as well as incorrect in reference to a standard variety of English.

Table 3.1 gives examples of the major types of unacceptable items that were identified. The syntactic items accounted for 48.24 per cent of the problem areas, the lexical items for 23.47 per cent and the stylistic items for 28.29 per cent.

All the informants agreed on the unacceptability of items listed under nominals, and determiners and modifiers. On the other hand, the Indian speakers did not generally judge the items under word order, verb patterns, or auxiliaries as unacceptable. There were, however, differences between native speaker groups. The British native speakers preferred the use of *would* or *should* in place of *will* and *shall* in requests such as 'I will be grateful if you could' and ' I shall appreciate if you would', whereas the American native speakers and Indian teachers did not object to these sentences. The Indian speakers, however, insisted on the use of *shall* with the first person and *will* elsewhere, although the native speakers did not object to the use of *will* with the first person. The three groups agreed on the unacceptability of the use of the present perfect in sentences 9 and 10, but the Indians did not object to the use of the present progressive in item 11. In general the three groups agreed about unacceptable forms of prepositions except in the specific cases of items 12 and 13, which the Indians found acceptable. The three groups also generally agreed about the

Table 3.1: 'Unacceptable' phrases in Indian English (adapted from Parasher 1994)

A Syntax

Nominals
Pluralization of nouns such as *equipments* and *evidences*

Determiners and modifiers
Use of singular count nouns such as *license* and *doctor* without an indefinite article

Word order
1   I will be definitely joining.
2   Cosmic ray methods also should be tried.

Verb patterns
3   We would appreciate if you could . . .
4   We suggest that immediate attention may be give to this.
5   I shall be obliged to have an early reply.

Auxiliaries
6   I would not be able to revise the draft.
7   I hope you might have received my letter.
8   We are doing what we can do.

Tense and aspect
9   Funds have been received last year.
10   As I have sent them two reminders last month.
11   We are manufacturing a malted food.

Prepositions
12   I am sorry to mention about my inability to . . .
13   We want to discuss about this programme.

Clause connectors and clause structure
14   Despatch the statement direct to the Personnel Department and in any case to reach them by 30 April.

B Lexis

15   We shall be highly obliged.
16   I shall be thankful if you . . .
17   The work on this project is yet to commence.
18   We invite your attention.
19   Kindly enhance our overdraft limit.
20   These are the charges for boarding and lodging.

Table 3.1: continued

21	We decided to bring out a separate journal with effect from January 1998.

C Style

22	Kindly please advise me.
23	I respectfully submit the following few lines for favour of your kind consideration.
24	With due respect I beg to inform you.
25	I have the honour to invite a reference to your letter
26	I need your esteemed help.

unacceptability of clause connector items such as the one in item 14. Examples listed under stylistic differences showed an interesting contrast. Whereas the native speaker groups found them to be overpolite, the Indian group did not.

The significant findings of the study are the generally high level of agreement among the three groups, the fact that on occasions even the native speaker groups differed, and the fact that the most striking differences between the native speakers and the Indian speakers related to items of lexis and style. Based on his findings, Parasher concludes,

> The results show that there were very few violations of the major rules of English syntax and none of these had a high frequency of occurrence. Moreover, there was practically no disagreement among the three informant groups in rejecting such expressions. It is in the deviant lexical and stylistic usage of IndE that its most characteristic features lie.
> (Parasher 1994: 163)

The study by Parasher is based on a corpus of texts written by educated Indian professionals who one would assume had a good command of standard Indian English. As was pointed out earlier, within most countries of the Outer Circle there is a cline among bilingual speakers of English. Studies that have investigated the use of English among individuals who would not be considered to be at the top level of English proficiency clearly demonstrate more use of so-called deviant features of English. A summary of one such study will illustrate the extent of syntactic variance on lower levels of the cline.

S. N. Sridhar (1996) sought to determine some of the syntactic patterns used by Indian students who were in their final year of formal training in

English. The corpus in this study consisted of in-class essays written by female students on the changing image of Indian women. All the students spoke Kannada as their first language. On average, they had studied English for 13 years, the majority of them in the context of an English medium education. Sridhar analyzed these essays in order to identify features that differed from native varieties of English. He found that in the majority of cases those structures that would be considered deviant were strikingly similar to corresponding structures in Kannada, the students' mother tongue.

There were numerous instances of literal transfer of idiomatic expressions from Kannada which, while not necessarily ungrammatical, would be considered unidiomatic, for example, 'In olden days, woman just worked like a bullock' and 'If her husband could die in her small age . . . '. Kannada often uses only one word to cover the meaning of two English words, for example, Kannada has only one word for *see* and *look*. This meant that sentences like the following occurred in the students' essays.

1 If we see only in the direction of art and literature . . .
2 Now, look the difference between . . .

Another feature that can be accounted for by transfer from the mother tongue is the use of *itself* as an emphatic particle regardless of the person, number, or gender of its antecedent, resulting in sentences like the following.

3 It must be due to the negligence of man or some fault of women itself.
4 If you falter in the first few steps itself . . .
5 But the woman then were not allowed to go out itself.

Whereas the majority of so-called deviant syntactic patterns contained in the essays can be explained by transfer, this was not true of all the items. For example, they contained a high number of sentences such as those given below, in which there was a lack of subject–verb agreement, even though verbs in Kannada agree in person, number, and gender with their subjects.

6 Akkamahadevi, a well-known poet in Kannada, have written a number of vacanas.
7 Now the present woman are seen in . . .
8 We must agree that all the Indian woman are not educated.

In light of the general richness of vocabulary and the broad range of syntactic patterns that he found, Sridhar maintains that the English used by these students could not be characterized as a pidgin or basilect. Rather he contends that it represents a variety that might be called a 'lower mesolect of South Asian English'.

Studies like Sridhar's raise the question of how changes in varieties of English come about. Are they solely a factor of transfer or are other processes involved? Such studies also raise the question of what criteria should be used in labeling syntactic patterns as standard when they are widely used but their acceptability is debatable. Sridhar (1996) maintains that at present these questions cannot be answered because current descriptions of indigenized varieties of English are vague and incomplete. As he says,

> The variability within each indigenized variety of English is so great—because of differences in schooling, proficiency, mother tongue, and functional range—that generalizations that apply to the prestigious or highly proficient users' variety do not necessarily apply to the varieties in the middle or lower range. It is, therefore, essential that generalization be stated relative to a lectal range, defined in terms of user characteristics (e.g. educational level, occupation, or mother tongue), structural criteria (phonological, morphological, lexical, syntactic, semantic, or pragmatic processes), and attitudinal evaluations ('standard', 'prestigious', etc.).
> (S. N. Sridhar 1996: 68)

The extent to which transfer from the mother tongue affects the development of indigenized varieties of English is a question that concerns a good deal of research on nativized varieties of English. Svalberg (1998), in her study of nativization in Brunei English, makes several important observations in this regard. Her study involved asking first-year university students to judge the grammaticality of tense and aspect in various English sentences. Some of these sentences included examples of tense and aspect use that are widely accepted in Brunei English but not in Standard English. Students were divided into high proficiency and low proficiency groups based on their English entry test results. Svalberg hypothesized that items not acceptable in Standard English that the majority of the high proficiency group deemed acceptable were part of an emerging pattern in Brunei English. Whereas for most of the example sentences, there was a clear difference in the judgment of the high proficiency group and the low proficiency group, Svalberg found a few sentences that were deemed acceptable by both the high and low groups. Two of these were the following:

1 Students are invited to the ceremony which would be held in the Staff-Student Centre.
2 As Ms. Edwards had broken her leg, class is cancelled today.

One possible explanation for the high acceptability of these sentences is that they represent structures that tend to be acquired late and thus they are simply learner errors. Svalberg, however, suggests that an equally plausible explanation is that the particular use of the past perfect in sentence 2 and of *would* in sentence 1 represent two features of an emerging Brunei English variety. As evidence for this position Svalberg examined selected editions of the local English language newspaper and found numerous examples of non-standard uses of both *would* and the past perfect. She also contends that some emerging features of Brunei English arise from what she terms a transfer of culture. For example, she believes that the non-standard use of *would* in present time contexts is motivated by desire of Brunei English speakers to lessen the assertiveness of their personal opinions.

It is debatable whether or not the use of sentences like those quoted above should be considered errors or part of an emerging Brunei variety. Selinker (1992) maintains that such sentences represent an *interlanguage*, that is, they represent a learner's unsuccessful attempts to acquire the standard forms of the language. Kachru (1994), on the other hand, maintains that the concept of interlanguage is not valid in reference to Outer Circle countries. This is because in order for a particular form to be considered an error and, hence, part of a learner's interlanguage, the learner must desire to emulate the standards of an Inner Circle country and, furthermore, must have the form readily available as a model in the social context in which they live. In the case of Brunei, forms promoted in Inner Circle countries such as particular uses of *would* and the past perfect may not be readily available and, even if they were, speakers of Brunei English may not desire to emulate them, preferring their own norms.

Furthermore, standards of use in Brunei, as in all Inner and Outer Circle countries, are constantly changing. Brunei English is influenced both by standards shared by Inner Circle countries and by those that develop in the local context. This has important pedagogical implications. As Svalberg (1998) points out in reference to the situation in Brunei,

> It is perhaps worth considering the implications of transfer from BNE [Brunei English] on the teaching of STE [Standard British English]. While transfer from Malay could be the main cause of deviations from what teachers see as 'basic' STE grammar norms, e.g. tense and number agreement, transfer from BNE may provide a better explanation for the exact form these deviations take and for their persistence. For English language educators, an awareness of the fact that proficient learners in Brunei have to master two varieties might in itself be helpful to both teachers and learners.
> (Svalberg 1998: 341)

Grammatical variation among different varieties of English has several important implications for the teaching of EIL. First, the examples presented above make it clear that only minor grammatical differences exist between standard nativized varieties of English and other standard varieties of English. Hence, for speakers of the standard nativized variety, there are few differences that will impede understanding between bilingual users of English and native speakers. Second, as was noted in the discussion of differences that do occur, it is extremely difficult to know when the use of a particular grammatical feature is an instance of learner error or part of an emerging feature of a standard nativized variety. Clearly, teachers who know the local standard nativized variety are in the best position to judge this. It is these teachers who can best advise their students as to when it would be appropriate to use a particular grammatical feature of the standard nativized variety.

What is perhaps most puzzling in the development of alternate standards in nativized varieties of English is the fact that whereas many educators accept lexical innovation as part of language change and recognize the legitimacy of such innovation, this tolerance is often not extended to grammatical innovation. In Widdowson's (1994) view, the reason for this lack of tolerance for grammatical variation is because grammar expresses a social identity. As he puts it, 'The mastery of a particular grammatical system, especially perhaps those features which are redundant, marks you as a member of the community which has developed that system for its own social purpose' (p. 381). Hence, when grammatical standards are challenged, they challenge the security of the community and institutions that support these standards. The use of particular grammatical features, however, is not the only way in which speakers of English can signal their membership of a specific speech community. The use of particular phonological patterns is in many ways an even more powerful way of demonstrating personal identity and group membership.

Phonological variation

The purpose of most studies of phonological variation in nativized varieties of English is to identify the unique segmental (consonants and vowels) and suprasegmental (e.g. stress and intonation) features of the variety. Tay (1982), for example, lists the particular features of Singaporean English in reference to acrolect, mesolect, and basilect speakers. Bamgboṣe (1992) distinguishes phonological features of Nigerian English, contending that while there are several phonetic features of Standard Nigerian English that reflect the first language background of the speakers, there are also general phonetic features that characterize the pronunciation of English by most Nigerians, regardless of their mother tongue.

Pandey (1994) describes the phonology of what he terms General Indian English, a description based on an investigation undertaken by the Central Institute of English and Foreign Language in Hyderabad. The purpose of this investigation was to describe the phonological features of English as it is spoken by individuals from different regions of India. According to Pandey, the motivation for the study developed from the fact that in India there has been a slow decline in the prestige of British Received Pronunciation (BRP) as a socially acceptable spoken variety, coupled with a growing belief that BRP is too ideal a model for Indian learners of English to acquire. Hence, the idea of describing a General Indian English pronunciation pattern that could be used for pedagogical purposes was developed. The description was to provide the basis for a pronunciation model that could be taught in formal education contexts as a way of assuring intelligibility between Indian English speakers and other English speakers both within and outside of the country.

In a related study, Agnihotri (1994) examined the sound patterns of Indian English from a sociolinguistic perspective. He contends that BRP is not a feasible model for acquisition in an Indian context, particularly because there is little motivation to acquire such it. As he says,

> In India, there is no pressure on the learners of English to speak RP; nor do they have any access to RP speakers, nor is their motivation strong enough to impel them to change their behaviour in the direction of RP. One wonders why most of the studies have evaluated their behaviour in terms of RP. If a variant of English is not stigmatized in the group to which its speaker belongs, he is not likely to change it whatever be the nature of inputs he may receive. (Agnihotri 1994: 241)

The studies by Pandey and Agnihotri lend support to the contention made earlier in the comparison of Singaporeans' and Indians' attitudes toward their own varieties of English that within India there appears to be a general acceptance of local norms as the target.

Whereas some Outer Circle countries like India prefer to use and promote local pronunciation patterns, this is not generally the case in the Expanding Circle countries. Rather in many of these countries there is a strong desire to acquire a native speaker variety of pronunciation. Dalton-Puffer, Kaltenboeck, and Smit (1997), for example, used a matched-guise test to investigate Austrian university students' attitudes toward three native accents of English (RP, near-RP, and General American) and two Austrian non-native accents of English. In general the study demonstrated the low status of Austrian accents and the students' preference for the native speaker variety with which they had become familiar in school or through travel. As the authors point out, even though students have a preference for native speaker models, these positive attitudes do not mean that they acquire them. The authors conclude that

successful L2 phonology learning thus cannot be attributed exclusively to the existence of positive attitudes towards the target accent. Clearly, there must be other factors exerting an influence on students' level of achievement.
(Dalton-Puffer *et al.* 1997: 126)

One of the factors that is likely to have a significant influence on students' use of local pronunciation patterns is their identification with a particular speech community. If individuals use English mainly within their own country or with other non-native speakers, it is likely that they will maintain English accents consistent with members of their own group.

As was pointed out at the beginning of the chapter, several definitions of Standard English suggest that a standard dialect can be spoken with any accent. The fact that there are many accepted accents used by native speakers of English supports this. However, in the case of non-native speaker accents, some educators advocate the acquisition of some degree of native speaker accent so as to ensure intelligibility. The issue of intelligibility is, of course, a particularly important point in reference to the study of EIL. How, then, can the conflict between the need to preserve international intelligibility and respect for the desire of some bilingual users of English to preserve their own identity as expressed in their pronunciation be resolved? One of the most balanced discussions of how to resolve this dilemma is provided by Jenkins (1998, 2000).

Jenkins (2000) maintains that in order to promote intelligibility in the use of EIL, which she restricts to interaction between two bilingual users of English, pronunciation classes should concentrate on those areas that appear to have the greatest influence on intelligibility, namely, particular segmentals, nuclear stress, and the effective use of articulatory setting. Other aspects of pronunciation could then be dealt with exclusively on the level of reception rather than production. As far as segmentals are concerned, Jenkins advocates focusing on specific core sounds, which include most consonant sounds, the distinction between long and short vowels, and consonant simplification. She also advocates emphasizing nuclear stress since this is so important in English in highlighting particular meaning, and provides the following example. In this sentence, the stress pattern of the first part is determined by the second:

Did you buy a tennis racket at the sports centre this morning, or
– was it a squash racket?
– did you buy it yesterday?
– did you only borrow one?
– was it your girlfriend who bought it?
– at the tennis club?
(Jenkins 2000: 153–4)

Finally, she advocates a focus on articulatory setting as this would enable learners to acquire both core sounds and nuclear stress. Articulatory settings involve the physical production of particular pronunciation features including such factors as tongue shape, differences in tension, and lip, cheek, and jaw posture.

Jenkins (2000) supports the view of intelligibility discussed earlier in the chapter in which it is seen as being 'dynamically negotiable between speaker and listener, rather than statically inherent in a speaker's linguistic forms' (p. 79). She argues that there is 'nothing intrinsically wrong with L2 pronunciation that does not conform to a NS [native speaker] accent but varies in the direction of the speaker's own L1' (p. 206) and maintains that such variation should not be equated with incorrectness if the accent is intelligible. She also advocates that phonology classes include extensive exposure to different varieties of English, particularly in the form of contrastive work, in order to help students recognize the differences between accents and thus enhance their receptive competence in EIL.

Perhaps the most valuable recommendation for teaching EIL pronunciation comes from Dalton and Seidlhofer (1994), who argue for the need to distinguish between norms and models. They contend that rather than approaching the teaching of a native speaker accent as the norm, it should be approached as a model that learners can use as a point of reference, preventing speakers of English from moving too far apart in their pronunciation.

As noted earlier, when educators discuss the issue of standards, they generally focus on grammatical differences and, to a lesser extent, on lexical and phonological variation, even though grammatical variation, especially on the acrolect level, has the least potential for causing problems of intelligibility. There are, however, two other areas of communicative competence that are often addressed in relation to standards, namely pragmatic and rhetorical competence. Discussions on standards in these areas, however, tend to focus primarily on the importance of promoting native speaker norms.

Pragmatic and rhetorical standards in English as an international language

Both pragmatic and rhetorical competence vary cross-culturally; both involve the speaker/writer or listener/reader in the meaning making process; and both entail a set of communicative purposes. Hence, it would make a good deal of sense to consider them together in relation to EIL.

However, because so much of the literature focuses on either spoken or written language, it is more straightforward to consider them separately. In the following discussion, we focus primarily on the issue of standards in relation to the teaching of pragmatic and rhetorical competence, arguing that typically a good deal of emphasis has been placed on achieving native speaker standards.

Pragmatic competence

Thomas's (1995) view of pragmatics as meaning in interaction is particularly productive in dealing with cross-cultural encounters because it emphasizes the fact that both speaker and listener must be involved in the meaning making process. As Thomas puts it,

> meaning is not something that is inherent in the words alone, nor is it produced by the speaker alone, nor by the hearer alone. Making meaning is a dynamic process, involving the negotiation of meaning between speaker and hearer, the context of utterance (physical, social and linguistic) and the meaning potential of an utterance.
> (Thomas 1995: 22)

Achieving *pragmatic competence* involves the ability to understand the *illocutionary force* of an utterance, that is, what a speaker intends by making it. This is particularly important in cross-cultural encounters since the same form (e.g. 'When are you leaving?') can vary in its illocutionary force depending on the context in which it is made (e.g. 'May I have a ride with you?' or 'Don't you think it is time for you to go?'). In cross-cultural encounters a speaker's intentions may not be understood by the listener. Pragmatic competence also involves the ability to know which form for expressing a particular meaning is most appropriate for a particular context (e.g. 'I need a lift.' versus 'Would it be possible to get a lift?'). Selecting a form that is not appropriate to the context can lead to cross-cultural misunderstandings.

In reference to EIL, two areas of pragmatics are particularly relevant, cross-cultural pragmatics and interlanguage pragmatics. Cross-cultural pragmatics investigates cultural differences in expectations regarding how particular speech acts should be enacted. Interlanguage pragmatics, on the other hand, deals specifically with the behavior of non-native speakers attempting to communicate in their second language. (For an excellent overview of existing research in interlanguage pragmatics, see Kasper and Rose 1999.)

A good deal of research in interlanguage pragmatics has assumed that transfer from speakers' first language/culture is what causes learners of a language to enact speech acts differently from native speakers of the language. Furthermore, it is often assumed that the goal of the L2 user of English is to achieve native-like pragmatic competence. Cohen (1996), for example, refers to the Cross-Cultural Speech Act Research Project (Blum-Kulka, House, and Kasper 1989) that compared the speech act behavior of native speakers of a variety of languages with the behavior of learners of those languages. For Cohen, the value of such studies is that they provide teachers and researchers with important information on how native speakers perform certain speech acts. In Cohen's view, this information should be used as a baseline to determine what should be done in the classroom. As he puts it,

> Once descriptions of the speech acts are made available, the next task is to determine the degree of control that learners have over those speech acts . . . Ideally, this information could then be used to prepare a course of instruction that would fill in the gaps in language knowledge and also give tips on strategies that might be useful for producing utterances. The role of the learners is to notice similarities and differences between the way native speakers perform such acts and the way they do.
> (Cohen 1996: 412)

However, a variety of problems exist in applying a native speaker model to the development of pragmatic competence. Kasper (1997) points out some of these difficulties. First, the so-called native speaker is not a homogeneous group. Even individuals within the same country and sharing a common culture can have different conversational styles. Furthermore, if, as was pointed out in Chapter 1, an international language is one that becomes de-nationalized, then there is no inherent reason why a native speaker model should inform the teaching of pragmatics in EIL. Second, according to Kasper, attempting to achieve native-like pragmatic competence, even if it were desirable, may not be a feasible goal for adult learners of English since, like phonology and syntax, pragmatic competence in an L2 may be increasingly difficult to acquire with age.

Kasper also suggests that in some cases language learners may lack the quality and quantity of contact with the second language that would give them the necessary input and occasions for gaining a high degree of pragmatic competence. Whereas the problem of a lack of L2 input may be true for many Expanding Circle countries, this is not the case in many Outer Circle countries. As was discussed in Chapter 2, bilingual users of English in Outer Circle countries often have specific contexts in which the language is used as the unmarked code for cross-cultural communication. In these circumstances, there are pragmatic rules that inform appropriate language use for particular contexts, and these are often not in keeping with so-called native speaker rules. Sridhar (1996b), for instance, in her study of requests within an Indian context, reports that her subjects had a high level of agreement as to what would be the appropriate use of English in particular contexts. For example, when asked to describe how they would ask a friend's mother for water if they were at their friend's home and very thirsty, many of the students indicated that they would wait for their friend to come back, or, if they did ask the mother, they would not use English but a combination of English and the mother tongue. Hence, in Outer Circle countries, bilingual users of English do not need to interact with native speakers to develop pragmatic competence for the appropriate use of English within their own country.

According to Kasper, another problem that exists in applying a native speaker model to the development of pragmatic competence is that, from the L2 learner's perspective, there may be sociopragmatic aspects of the target culture that conflict with his or her beliefs and values. Sridhar (1996b), for example, found that Indian speakers when making requests in English within India often used forms that would be considered overly polite by native speaker judges. If most Indian speakers believe that such formality is warranted within their own sociocultural context, then it is unreasonable to require that these speakers use forms that so-called native speakers would use simply because English has the status of an inter-national language. Finally, for Kasper, a native speaker model is often not appropriate since native-like pragmatic competence in bilingual users of English may be viewed negatively by some native speakers in the target culture. In fact, some studies suggest that there may be benefits in not conforming to native speaker pragmatics.

Aston (1993), for example, suggests that not having native-like competence may be a means of establishing friendly relationships—or what he terms *comity*—between people of different cultures. In order to achieve solidarity and support in cross-cultural contexts, Aston contends that people need to focus on their identities as individuals rather than as representatives of members of their culture of origin. If this is done, then they can achieve comity by, for example, expressing a critical stance toward their own country, or exploiting their own incompetence in either the language or specific areas of knowledge. For Aston, the potential to establish comity in cross-cultural encounters

> supports the argument that interlanguage pragmatics should operate with a difference hypothesis rather than a deficit hypothesis . . . and not simply analyze NNS discourse in terms of failure to conform to NS conversational norms. Pedagogically, it implies that the learner's task in developing an ability for interactional speech using the L2 is not simply one of acquiring native-like sociolinguistic competence in the attempt to mimic the behavior of a native speaker, but requires

the development of an ability to use specific comity strategies appropriate to the context of NNS discourse.
(Aston 1993: 245)

In discussing alternatives to applying a native speaker model when teaching
pragmatic competence, it is useful to separate the use of English within
Outer Circle countries from its use by individuals from other countries. In
the former case, it is evident from our discussion of codeswitching in
Kenya in Chapter 2 that speakers who use English within their own
country have a clear sense of when and how to use it appropriately in
particular social encounters. For these purposes, an individual's pragmatic
competence is developed as he or she uses English in their everyday
encounters. In the use of EIL between individuals from different countries,
whereas there is little reason to advocate a native speaker model, there are
some pedagogical strategies that may be helpful in developing productive
cross-cultural communication. The first is to raise the awareness of both
native speakers and bilingual users of English that pragmatic rules can
differ significantly cross-culturally. The second is to stress the variety of
ways in which speakers from various backgrounds can work to establish
comity in cross-cultural encounters.

In closing our discussion on pragmatic competence, it is interesting to note
that there is some evidence to suggest (see Bardovi-Harlig and Dörnyei
1998) that for bilingual users of English in Expanding Circle countries,
pragmatic violations are considered to be less serious than grammatical
violations. This may be due to the fact that, for many bilingual users of
English, the implications of not achieving grammatical competence are
more serious than those of not achieving pragmatic competence since
success in many gatekeeping examinations rests on grammatical accuracy.

Rhetorical competence

Rhetorical competence, as it relates to the use of EIL, has been investigated
in studies of *contrastive rhetoric* (for an overview, see Connor 1996; Leki
1991). Connor defines contrastive rhetoric as 'an area of research in second
language acquisition that identifies problems in composition encountered
by second language writers, and, by referring to the rhetorical strategies of
the first language, attempts to explain them' (1996: 5). Hence, contrastive
rhetoric, like interlanguage pragmatics, attempts to explain bilingual
English users' 'problems' in using English by comparing their rhetorical
patterns to those of native speakers, suggesting that native speaker
discourse is the target for bilingual users. This is an assumption which, as
was suggested above in the discussion of pragmatic competence, needs to
be questioned.

Some researchers in contrastive rhetoric have proposed that the writers from particular cultures tend to have a specific culturally influenced relationship with their readers. Hinds (1987), for example, posits that written texts in many western cultures can be characterized as 'writer responsible' since it is the writers' responsibility to ensure that effective communication takes place by directly stating their intentions. In other cultures, however, it is the reader who is responsible for determining the writer's primary intent. This distinction has reinforced the notion, first described by Kaplan (1966), that western writing tends to be direct, whereas a good deal of writing in eastern countries is indirect in that the main point is often never stated and hence must be inferred by the reader.

Ballard and Clanchy (1991) argue that the majority of rhetorical differences develop from specific cultural approaches to learning. They contend that in many Asian countries, learning strategies often entail memorization and imitation, resulting in an approach to learning that encourages the conservation of existing knowledge. On the other hand, they maintain that many western cultures encourage a speculative or critical approach to learning, resulting in an extension of existing knowledge. As a result, writers in the west are encouraged to present their own opinion on a particular topic as they speculate about the various possibilities contained in the issue. However, such generalizations regarding eastern and western approaches to knowledge and learning are highly inadequate and can have many negative repercussions, as I will argue in Chapter 5.

Contrastive rhetoric has been a primary focus in the teaching of writing to bilingual users of English in Inner Circle countries. In this context there has been a major debate as to whether or not bilingual users should be required to accommodate to the rhetorical patterns of the Inner Circle country in which they are studying, or if they should be allowed—or even encouraged—to organize their written texts according to the rhetorical patterns of their first language. Many argue that if students are to succeed academically in a western context, they must acquire the ways of organizing discourse that prevail in the west (see, for example, Reid 1994; Ballard and Clanchy 1991). Others, however, maintain that in demanding that second language writers should acquire a particular rhetorical pattern, educators are asking them to accept western cultural patterns of textual development. Land and Whitley, for example, maintain that asking second language writers to use a deductive linear argument when they write in English is basically a matter of colonization. As they put it,

> By asking these students to use our signals according to our expectations, we are not taking language to be a 'system of abstract grammatical categories'; instead we are at least implicitly

> understanding 'language conceived as ideologically saturated, language as world view' (Bakhtin 1975/1981: 271). We require our ESL students to share and reproduce in their writing our world view, one to which they are, of course, alien. Such instruction is composition as colonization.
> (Land and Whitley 1989: 289)

If we examine written texts from an EIL perspective, it is important to consider to what extent using culturally different rhetorical patterns to organize English texts can result in a lack of intelligibility. Unfortunately, most existing research in contrastive rhetoric has sought to determine the features by which texts differ on the basis of cultural patterns rather than investigating how these differences affect comprehension. Clearly this is an area in which research is needed. Meanwhile, as with pragmatic competence, it is useful to separate the use of EIL in Outer Circle countries and its use in an international context. In the former case, there is no question that rhetorical patterns commonly used within the culture are the best ones to teach. In the case of English in internationally circulated journals, if, as we stated in the opening chapters, an essential characteristic of EIL is that it is de-nationalized, then it is unclear why largely western modes of rhetorical development should be exclusively used in such journals. It may well be that readers of EIL need to be, in Hind's terminology, reader-responsible and contribute more to the reading process.

Summary

In this chapter we have explored the issue of standards in reference to variation in present-day English. We began with a discussion of the various definitions of Standard English and highlighted the problems that exist in trying to determine when a particular feature can be considered standard. Frequently those who support the promotion of Standard English argue that if consistent standards are not upheld, there will be a loss of intelligibility among speakers of English. Others argue that this possibility is unlikely due to the fact that many speakers of English in the Outer Circle acquire the language in a formal educational context where standards of use are promoted. Finally, some question why innovation is allowed in Inner Circle contexts, yet there is little tolerance for innovation among bilingual users of English.

Whereas many individuals accept lexical innovations, viewing them as part of the creativity of language use, the examples included in the chapter demonstrate that lexical variation can result in problems of comprehension when the context of use does not make the meaning clear. The discussion of grammatical features demonstrated that the extent of variation in grammatical standards is dependent on whether the variety is an acrolect, mesolect, or basilect. On an acrolect level, most grammatical differences are minor, and there exists widespread agreement regarding what is considered to be acceptable usage. The extent of grammatical differences on other levels is generally related to a speaker's education, mother tongue, and proficiency in English. A central concern in approaching grammatical variation is whether or not a particular usage reflects an error on the part of the speaker or rather a feature that will become accepted in the local nativized variety of English.

Transfer from the mother tongue accounts for many features of the phonological patterns of specific varieties of English. However, there are features that are typical of speakers in a country regardless of their mother tongue, and local phonological patterns are often important in signaling a speaker's speech community and linguistic identity. Nevertheless, in terms of attitudes, many bilingual users of English still regard a native speaker model of pronunciation as having greatest prestige.

In the discussions on pragmatic and rhetorical competence we examined the problems that exist in using a native speaker model as a target. We argued that attention to pragmatic competence should focus on developing an awareness of cross-cultural variation in spoken interactions rather than promoting Inner Circle pragmatic rules. In the case of rhetorical competence, we summarized some of the research findings of contrastive rhetoric that demonstrate the manner in which textual development can differ cross-culturally. We maintained that the use of EIL should not be associated with any particular rhetorical tradition and emphasized the need for readers of English to be willing to process English texts that conform to a variety of rhetorical patterns.

The discussions on pragmatic and rhetorical competence highlighted the relationship that exists between language and culture. In the next two chapters we will explore this more fully, focusing on how culture is relevant to the choice of topics used in the teaching of English and in the methods adopted. We will argue that if an international language is one that by definition belongs to no one particular country or culture, then there are valid reasons for promoting local cultural topics and ways of learning.

Further reading

On standards and Standard English

Bamgboṣe, A. 1998. 'Torn between the norms: innovations in world Englishes.' *World Englishes* 17/1: 1–14.

Brutt-Griffler, J. 1998. 'Conceptual questions in English as a world language: taking up an issue.' *World Englishes* 17/3: 381–92.

Kachru, B. B. 1985. 'Standards, codification and sociolinguistic realism: the English language in the outer circle' in Quirk, R. and H. G. Widdowson (eds): *English in the World: Teaching and Learning the Language and Literatures.* Cambridge: Cambridge University Press: 11–30.

Quirk, R. 1985. 'The English language in a global context' in Quirk, R. and H. G. Widdowson (eds): *English in the World: Teaching and Learning the Language and Literatures.* Cambridge: Cambridge University Press: 1–6.

Quirk, R. 1990. 'What is standard English?' in Quirk, R. and G. Stein (eds): *English in Use.* London: Longman: 112–25.

On lexical, grammatical, and phonological variation

Butler, S. 1996. 'World English in an Asian context: the Macquarie dictionary project.' *World Englishes* 15/3: 347–57.

Jenkins, J. 1998. 'Which pronunciation norms and models for English as an international language?' *ELT Journal* 52/2: 119–26.

Jenkins, J. 2000. *The Phonology of English as an International Language.* Oxford: Oxford University Press.

Parasher, S. V. 1994. 'Indian English: certain grammatical, lexical and stylistic features' in Angihotri, R. K. and A. L. Khanna (eds): *Second Language Acquisition: Socio-Cultural and Linguistic Aspects of English in India.* New Delhi: Sage Publications: 145–64.

Shastri, S. V. 1996. 'Using computer corpora in the description of language with special reference to complementation in Indian English' in Baumgardner, R. J. (ed.): *South Asian English.* Chicago: University of Illinois Press: 70–81.

Sridhar, S. N. 1996. 'Toward a syntax of South Asian English: defining the lectal range' in Baumgardner, R. J. (ed.): *South Asian English.* Chicago: University of Illinois Press: 55–69.

On pragmatic and rhetorical competence

Connor, U. 1996. *Contrastive Rhetoric: Cross-cultural Aspects of Second-Language Writing.* Cambridge: Cambridge University Press.

Kaplan, R. 1966. 'Cultural thought patterns in inter-cultural education.' *Language Learning* 16: 1–20.

Kasper, G. 1997. 'The role of pragmatics in language teacher education' in Bardovi-Harlig, K. and B. Hartford (eds): *Beyond Methods.* New York: McGraw-Hill Company: 113–41.

Thomas, J. 1995. *Meaning in Interaction: An Introduction to Pragmatics.* London: Longman.

4 CULTURE IN TEACHING ENGLISH AS AN INTERNATIONAL LANGUAGE

In this chapter we explore the role of culture in EIL teaching in terms of the cultural content of teaching materials and in reference to the use of EIL in specific discourse communities. In the case of teaching materials, we focus on what cultural information is taught in EIL classrooms: in the case of discourse communities, we focus on the way in which sociocultural practices influence how texts are developed and used.

The use of cultural content in EIL teaching is problematic in light of the assumptions that were made in Chapter 1 regarding the characteristics of an international language. In the case of English, these are that:

1 As it is an international language, the use of English is no longer connected to the culture of Inner Circle countries.
2 One of the primary functions of English, as is the case with any international language, is to enable speakers to share their ideas and cultures.

I will argue that one of the primary reasons for dealing with cultural content in EIL teaching is because the use of EIL involves crossing borders, both literally and figuratively, as individuals interact in cross-cultural encounters. The chapter begins by considering the role of culture in language teaching materials. In this section I emphasize that culture learning is a social process and that, in reference to EIL, understanding one's own culture in relation to that of others is paramount. We then explore various rationales for the inclusion of culture learning in the language classroom, including the idea of culture as motivating content. This is followed by an examination of whose culture should be included in an EIL classroom. Here, we examine the benefits and disadvantages that arise from using cultural content from the local culture, a target culture, or a more general international culture. Various strategies that can be used to promote a reflective approach to culture are then suggested. The final section of the chapter examines how the discourse of various communities is informed by specific cultural values that cut across the primary cultures of ethnicity and geography.

The role of culture in language teaching

Culture in language teaching has traditionally involved providing cultural information. Such information typically includes at least one of the following dimensions of culture discussed by Adaskou, Britten, and Fahsi (1990): 'the aesthetic sense' in which the literature, film, and music of a target language country are examined; 'the sociological sense' in which the customs and institutions of this country are explained; 'the semantic sense' in which how a culture's conceptual system is embodied in a language is investigated; and 'the pragmatic sense' in which how cultural norms influence what language is appropriate for which contexts is examined.

Two major problems exist with this approach to culture in relation to the teaching of EIL. First, as was pointed out in the introduction to this chapter, it cannot be assumed that the culture of any one particular country, especially an Inner Circle country, should provide the basis for cultural content when teaching EIL. Second, if one of the goals of using culture in EIL teaching is to help individuals interact in cross-cultural encounters, then merely knowing about a culture will not be sufficient to gain insight into how to interact in these encounters. In order for this to occur, learners need to reflect on how such information might affect their interaction. But how can this kind of reflection be encouraged in an EIL classroom? In order to answer this question, it is helpful to consider how cultural information is acquired outside of a classroom and how this type of cultural learning might be encouraged within it.

Spradley (1980), a noted ethnographer, maintains that culture involves three fundamental aspects of human experience: what people do (cultural behavior), what people know (cultural knowledge), and what things people make and use (cultural artifacts). He argues that individuals acquire knowledge about these various aspects of culture by interacting with one another; for example, they have meanings for things they encounter, but those meanings may be modified as they interact with others. Culture then is 'the knowledge that people have learned as members of a group' (Spradley 1980: 10).

If culture outside of the classroom is acquired by means of individuals interacting with one another, how can a classroom become an extension of this process and students be encouraged to reflect on and perhaps modify the meaning they have for things they encounter? Two goals discussed by Kramsch (1993) regarding culture in language teaching are particularly relevant here.

1 Establishing a 'sphere of interculturality': this line of thought promotes the idea that the learning of culture is more than just the transfer of information between cultures. Rather, learning about a culture requires

that an individual consider his or her own culture in relation to another. Hence, the process of learning about another culture entails a reflection on one's own culture as well as the target culture.

2 Teaching culture as difference: this notion of culture highlights the fact that national identities are not monolithic. Within each culture there exists a variety of national characteristics that are related to age, gender, regional origin, ethnic background, and social class.

Let us consider how both of these goals are valuable in approaching culture in EIL teaching. Since, as was argued in Chapter 1, one of the major reasons for using EIL is to enable speakers to share their ideas and culture with others in cross-cultural encounters, it is beneficial for learners to be asked to reflect on their own culture in relation to others, or, as Kramsch puts it, to establish a sphere of interculturality. This requires two essential steps. First, learners need to acquire knowledge about another culture and then they need to reflect on how their own culture contrasts with it. In acquiring knowledge about and reflecting on another culture, like Spradley (1980), I would argue for the importance of not assuming that the meaning particular cultural behavior has for the members of one group is the same as it has for others. Spradley argues that in trying to understand another culture, one of first things an individual must do is to put aside what he terms 'naïve realism', the idea that all people define the real world in pretty much the same way, that love, worship, food, death, and so on all have similar meanings for everyone. In line with this assumption, one goal that should be encouraged when asking students to reflect on another culture is for them to consider what meaning particular behavior might have for members of that culture, and not to assume that it is the same as the one they have.

Teaching culture as difference is also important because of the common use of EIL in cross-cultural encounters. Frequently, the introduction of cultural content in language teaching encourages what Atkinson terms a 'received view of culture', that is, a view of culture 'as geographically (and quite often nationally) distinct entities, as relatively unchanging and homogeneous, and as all-encompassing systems of rules or norms that substantially determine personal behavior' (1999: 626). In using EIL in cross-cultural encounters students need to be encouraged not to adopt this view but rather to recognize the diversity that exists within all cultures, particularly in the modern era of travel and migration when cultures are in constant contact. Atkinson argues for a middle ground in approaching culture in language teaching in which educators, while recognizing 'the important place of shared perspectives and socialized practices in the lives of human beings' (p. 610), nevertheless acknowledge that no two people share exactly the same set of experiences or views of the world and hence no two people can be said to share exactly the same culture. Later in the chapter we will explore in detail how these two perspectives—establishing a sphere of interculturality and teaching culture as difference—can be encouraged in an EIL classroom.

Learning about another culture does not necessarily mean that one must accept that culture. Kramsch (1993), for example, argues that knowing about a culture (gaining cultural competence) does not mean that one has an obligation to behave in accordance with its conventions. Thus, as was noted in the previous chapter, whereas an individual may learn about pragmatic differences that exist between cultures, the goal of EIL teaching should not be for students to accept the standards of Inner Circle countries, but rather to recognize how particular pragmatic differences might affect their own cross-cultural encounters. Byram (1998) makes a similar distinction between knowing about another culture and accepting another culture when he distinguishes what he terms 'biculturalism' and 'interculturalism'. For Byram, biculturalism assumes that an individual identifies with and accepts the beliefs, values, and practices of a particular culture. Interculturalism, on the other hand, assumes a knowledge of rather than acceptance of another culture. In becoming bicultural an individual would seek to acquire, for example, a culture's pragmatic rules. In the case of interculturalism, on the other hand, an individual would seek only to gain knowledge of these rules. To acquire an international language, which, as we have argued consistently, belongs to its users, clearly does not require biculturalism.

Rationales for culture learning

It can be questioned whether the teaching of culture is necessary to the teaching of an international language such as English, which has become de-nationalized and no longer belongs to Inner Circle countries. Indeed, there are those who argue that there is no need to include culture in the teaching of EIL. González, for example, maintains that in the teaching of English as an International Auxiliary Language (EIAL), 'English is deracinated or uprooted from its original cultural soil; only special registers of science and technology, business and geopolitics are used' (1995: 58). Central to his argument is the assumption that teaching EIL is nothing more than teaching English for specific purposes (ESP). Brutt-Griffler, for one, disputes this notion, pointing out that

> when we say that people in the Outer and Expanding Circle are English-using, we must admit at least the possibility that they may use English for all the purposes to which a language may be put. (Brutt-Griffler 1998: 389)

Hence, the fact that an individual may initially acquire English to serve a specific purpose does not mean that he or she is then confined to using English for that purpose. Rather the ability to speak the language allows individuals the possibility of using it to achieve a variety of communicative goals.

However, even if one accepts the notion that EIL is essentially English for specific purposes, some people would argue that cultural values are present in this use of the language. Brown (1990), for example, points out that within scientific writing there are many cultural assumptions and presuppositions regarding, for instance, the nature of objectivity, the importance of truthfulness in scientific endeavors, and what is appropriate to include or exclude in a scientific report. This is a point we will examine in more detail later in the chapter. If all uses of EIL, including English for Specific Purposes (ESP), entail some cultural dimension, it would appear that one cannot avoid the issue of culture in the teaching of English. Indeed, Valdes is one of many who maintains that 'it is virtually impossible to teach a language without teaching cultural content' (1986: 121). So if culture is essential to the teaching of a language, the question is: in what ways is it essential?

One answer to this question, indicated above, is that in order to use English for special purposes, an individual needs to acquire the culturally influenced ways of using particular discourse. This is an important rationale for including the teaching of culture in an EIL classroom. Another rationale, proposed by Brown (1986), is that culture is necessary because 'it is really an integral part of the interaction between language and thought. Cultural patterns, customs, and ways of life are expressed in language; culture-specific world views are reflected in language' (p. 45).

The question in relation to EIL is which particular culturally influenced uses of English do learners need to acquire? As was pointed out in Chapter 3, lexical innovation are occurring in the development of many nativized varieties of English. These innovations often provide a means to describe a cultural aspect of local life, for example the use of *clansmen* in Hong Kong or *minor wife* in Thailand. But is it necessary to know these words in order to be considered a user of English? I would argue that if an international language is one that is de-nationalized, then there is no reason why bilingual users of English need to acquire the localized lexical items of any country other than their own.

Lexical items that include cultural knowledge exist on a continuum. Some need to be acquired because of their frequent use in international contexts, whereas others are more restricted to use in a particular locality or country. To take the example of the United States, readers might come across terms such as 'The Big Three', 'big stick diplomacy', or 'yellow journalism', all terms that have emerged from the historical and political development of the country. Because of their local meaning, these phrases are not central to the learning of EIL. On the other hand, there are terms that have emerged from more general western traditions such as 'Pandora's box', 'the Midas touch', or 'the good Samaritan' that are perhaps more relevant to EIL. Hence, a difficult question in EIL teaching is to define the parameters of global as opposed to local lexical knowledge. One principle may be that the more locally used the lexical item, and the lower its frequency the less likely it will be needed in the use of EIL.

While some people argue for the inclusion of culture in language teaching on the basis that one cannot acquire the language without an understanding of the culture or cultures with which it is associated, others argue for the inclusion of information about specific cultures on the grounds that cultural content in general is motivating to students. Richards (1995), for example, in developing a textbook project, surveyed Japanese students about their life and interests in order to select content that would be motivating for the students. The survey results showed that the students wanted to deal with cultural content and to learn primarily about the United States, followed by Britain and China. More specifically, they were most curious about school life in the United States, American food, American music, and American films. However, they were also very interested in Americans' opinions of Japan. The survey is interesting in that it illustrates that what students, at least these Japanese university students, want to know about most is cultural artifacts—for example food, music, and films. But if topics are presented in terms of information about a specific culture, they do little to further the type of reflection that is necessary in establishing a sphere of interculturality so essential to the use of EIL.

Although many people support the inclusion of culture in language teaching on the grounds that it is motivating, others dispute the value of cultural content in this regard. Prodromou (1992), for example, surveyed Greek students, mostly young adults, studying in private language institutes and at a British Council Teaching Centre as to what they believed should be the subject matter of English lessons. The two most popular topics were 'the English language' and 'science and society'. The students' reaction to cultural content was mixed. Whereas 60 per cent wanted to study British life and institutions, only about 25 per cent wanted to study either American or Greek life and institutions. Prodromou hypothesized that the students' interest in British life and institutions might be due to a belief that if they knew more about British life, they would do better in the British-based Cambridge exam. If this is the case, overall these students did not find learning about culture, either their own or others, very motivating.

Prodromou (1988) maintains that one reason students are not motivated by culture learning is the way culture is presented in many ELT textbooks. He maintains that globally designed textbooks have continued to be stubbornly Anglo-centric:

> appealing to a world market as they do, they cannot by definition draw on local varieties of English and have not gone very far in recognizing English as an international language either. What were they about? They were mostly about situations which were not only imaginary . . . but vacuous, empty of life. Even when the textbooks went technicolour, they were still marketing a black-and-white cardboard cut-out world.
> (Prodromou 1988: 76)

Prodromou maintains that when students enter the language classroom,

> they leave their three-dimensional humanity outside and enter the plastic world of efl textbooks; textbooks where life is safe and innocent, and does not say or do anything. Our modern books are full of speech acts that don't act, don't mean anything . . . Most textbooks project an Anglo-centric, male-dominated, middle-class utopia of one kind or another.
> (Prodromou 1988: 79)

Thus, he maintains, it is understandable why students find little to motivate them in the foreign language class. He argues that when 'both the material we use and the way we use it are culturally alienating then, inevitably, the students switch off, retreat into their inner world, to defend their own integrity' (ibid.: 80).

Adaskou, Britten, and Fahsi (1990) also question the notion that the inclusion of cultural information, specifically that relating to the target culture, is motivating to students, in this case Moroccan students. Drawing on interviews with Moroccan teachers, they note that, in general, the teachers believe that including information about the target culture contributes to students' discontent with their own material culture by inviting comparisons. The teachers also maintain that there are patterns of behavior that exist in Britain and America that many Moroccans would prefer that their young people do not see. Finally, the teachers believe that students will be more, not less, motivated to learn English if the language is presented in contexts that relate to their own lives as young adults rather than to see it presented in the context of an English-speaking country.

These mixed findings regarding the motivating influence of cultural content suggest that the debate whether or not to include it in the ELT classroom has less to do with whether or not to include culture and more to do with what to include. This is the topic to which we now turn.

Cultural content in language teaching materials

Cortazzi and Jin (1999) distinguish three types of cultural information that can be used in language textbooks and materials:

- 'source culture materials' that draw on the learners' own culture as content
- 'target culture materials' that use the culture of a country where English is spoken as a first language
- 'international target culture materials' that use a great variety of cultures in English- and non-English-speaking countries around the world.

As we argued at the beginning of the chapter, culture teaching in EIL needs to be more than supplying information about various cultures if it is to be helpful in using the language for both cross-cultural encounters and sharing insights about one's own culture with others. In order to develop these uses of EIL, students need to be encouraged to reflect on their own culture in relation to others as a way of establishing a sphere of inter-culturality. What cultural content to include is only part of the issue. Equally important is how to deal with this content in a particular context. Because EIL today is taught in such a wide variety of contexts, involving teachers and students from various cultural backgrounds and textbooks that include information on different cultures, it is necessary to consider how these various dynamics can be used to establish a sphere of inter-culturality and contribute to students' use of EIL in cross-cultural encounters.

Target culture materials

Figure 4.1 illustrates two possible contexts in which information about a target culture can be introduced in the teaching of EIL. One very common context today, which typically occurs in Expanding Circle countries, is where the teacher and students come from the same cultural background, but the materials used in the classroom present cultural information from a target culture. This would be the case, for example, in a classroom in Thailand with a Thai teacher using materials dealing with American culture. Whereas it is possible, as noted above, that content relating to the target culture may be motivating to some students, a more important

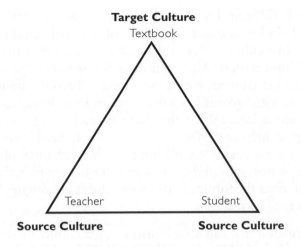

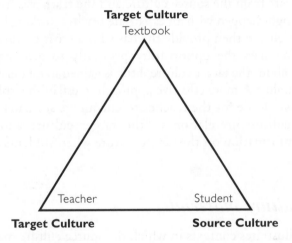

Figure 4.1: Two contexts in which information about a target culture can be introduced in an EIL classroom

concern in relation to the teaching of EIL is how such a context can be used productively to establish a sphere of interculturality.

It may be, as suggested earlier, that some of the cultural content relating to the target culture, or cultures, is largely irrelevant or uninteresting to some of the students, or even presents cultural conflicts. For example, a discussion of garage sales may be irrelevant to students who do not have such sales in their own country; shoes placed inside western homes may be puzzling to students who come from cultures where shoes stay outside of the home. One Korean teacher I worked with told me about his experience using a book published in America with his class in Korea. In one exercise in the book, students were asked to look at photographs of various American scenes depicting different periods of history and decide in which decade the picture was taken. As one might imagine, students found the task extremely difficult. Furthermore, he as teacher had few resources to draw on to help his students. This kind of material could be especially problematic in a culture where the teacher is considered to be the main provider of information. Also, it is doubtful whether the material was relevant in an EIL context, where the language becomes de-nationalized and the educational goal is to enable learners to communicate to others their ideas and culture. What this Korean teacher did was to seize the opportunity to help students learn more about their own culture, an important component of establishing a sphere of interculturality. He replaced the photographs in the text with some of various periods in Korea and then followed the format in the book, thus encouraging his students to reflect on their own culture.

A second situation that can arise in using target culture materials is when the students are from the source culture and the teacher is from the target culture, as might happen with an expatriate teacher working in China. The classroom itself can then provide the basis for a cross-cultural encounter. If the teacher uses the opportunity primarily to give students more information about the target culture, little is gained in establishing a sphere of interculturality. A more effective approach to establish a sphere of inter-culturality would be for the teacher to encourage students to reflect on their own culture in relation to the target culture and to provide additional information on the target culture when students request such information.

Source culture materials

Figure 4.2 illustrates contexts in which the source culture may be used in an EIL classroom. In the first case, the students, teacher, and text all share the source culture. For example, a textbook published and used in Japan with Japanese students and teacher might ask the students to describe annual Japanese events like the Children's Day Festival and the Moon-Viewing Festival and traditional arts like Haiku, Noh comedy, and Bunraku puppet shows. Clearly such a context provides the students with an opportunity to learn more about their own culture and to learn the language needed to explain these cultural elements in English, but can it contribute to establishing a sphere of interculturality in which they consider their own culture in relation to another? The teacher could exploit the material by asking individual students to describe what specific aspects of their culture mean to them as a way of demonstrating the variance that exists within one culture and promoting a view of culture as difference. The teacher could also use material relating to the source culture in ways that encourage students to consider how they would explain elements of their own culture to others.

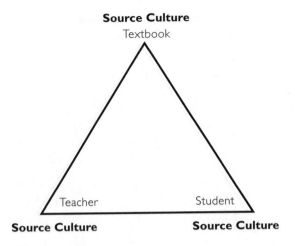

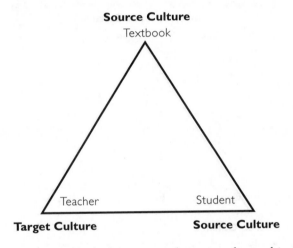

Figure 4.2: Contexts in which the source culture may be used in an EIL classroom

Source culture texts can also be used in contexts where the students come from the source culture but the teacher is from another culture. In such a situation, the teacher, if not familiar with some of the cultural topics, can become an interested listener, creating an ideal context for establishing a sphere of interculturality. The teacher might pose questions to the students, asking them to explain what meaning a particular cultural element has for them, and share with students his or her personal reaction to the cultural information and behavior presented in the text.

International target culture materials

Figure 4.3 shows two contexts in which international target culture materials representing many English and non-English speaking countries

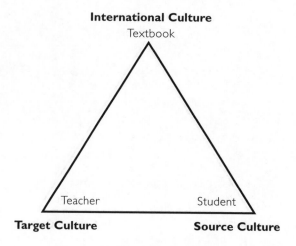

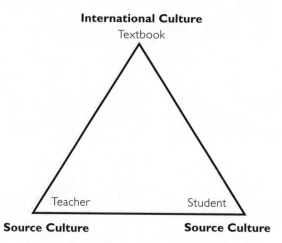

Figure 4.3: Two contexts in which international target culture might be used in an EIL *classroom*

might be used. When both the students and the teacher come from a culture not represented in the text, as could occur in both contexts, that is with a teacher from the source culture and with an expatriate teacher, many of the same problems discussed in reference to the use of a target culture could occur. Students may be uninterested or puzzled by the information in the text, and teachers may not have access to additional information needed to explain some of the cultural references. This may result in no one in the class being able to comment on the culture presented; hence the degree of understanding both teacher and students can gain about the culture presented in the text will be limited.

Are there any potential benefits from using content from an international target culture? This depends on what cultural information is included and how it is presented. One value of this kind of material is that it can illustrate the diverse contexts in which English is used as an international language. Imagine a text in which bilingual users interact with other speakers of English in cross-cultural encounters for a variety of purposes. Such materials could have several benefits. For example, they could exemplify the manner in which English can be used internationally, or they could include examples of lexical, grammatical, and phonological variation in context. They could also illustrate cross-cultural pragmatics in which bilingual users of English draw on their own rules of appropriateness. They could then provide a basis for students to gain a fuller understanding of how English today serves a great variety of international purposes in a broad range of contexts, thus encouraging students to reflect on their own local and global uses of EIL.

The above discussion demonstrates that an assessment of whose culture to use in teaching EIL needs to be made in the context of specific classrooms and the dynamics that exist among the teacher, students, and textbook. In all contexts it is important to consider how a sphere of interculturality can be encouraged.

A reflective approach to cultural content

One of the first steps that needs to be taken in approaching the cultural content used in an EIL class is to examine in what ways it might appear unusual to members of another culture. Let us take, for example, a lesson on garage sales that is presented in the context of asking for and giving advice (Hynes and Baichman 1989). The chapter opens with the following information and instructions.

> A garage sale is a sale of items you no longer want or need. People have these sales in their homes, yards, or garages. It is a way for sellers to make money by getting rid of old items. It is also a way for buyers to get secondhand items, or used items, cheaply.

> Look at the list below. With a partner decide which items you would want to buy new and which items you wouldn't mind buying secondhand. Write *N* or *S*. Then discuss your answers with your classmates.
> (Hynes and Baichman 1989: 47)

Students are then asked to check the following items: a cassette recorder, shoes, pots and pans, a mattress, children's toys, a rocking chair, sheets, blankets and pillows, a clock radio, babies' clothes, old records, pictures with frames, a tablecloth, jewelry, a toaster, a rug, underwear, a winter coat, and tools. The chapter then continues with a character named Janina asking another named Roberto whether or not he thinks she should have the sale on Saturday or Sunday, whether or not she should put an ad in the paper or put signs up in the neighborhood, and whether or not she should put signs in the front yard or backyard. The unit ends by asking students to think of some advice they need, ask a partner for this advice, and then decide whether or not they would take this advice.

For those from cultures in which garage sales are held, the cultural information appears rather innocuous, although it is important to point out that personal reactions to the value of garage sales would vary tremendously among members of these cultures. For those from other cultures, however, there may be a good deal that is puzzling. If, for example, this particular text were to be used in Iran, many things might be quite unfamiliar to the students. When household items are sold in Iran, they are generally sold indoors in the seller's home and buyers often call and make an appointment to go and look at them. Also, some Iranian students could be surprised—and perhaps offended—by the idea of buying used mattresses, sheets, blankets, and underwear and they might be puzzled by the selling of pictures with frames since in Iran pictures are private items and pictures of family members particularly would never be displayed in a sale. As far as the exercise on giving advice is concerned, this might appear unusual to some students since in Iran it is not customary to put signs in the neighborhood.

As was pointed out earlier in our discussion of the role of culture in language learning, it is extremely important to recognize the great diversity that exists within any culture. Thus, within any classroom in Iran there would no doubt be mixed reactions to the text, depending on individual students' familiarity with garage sales both within their own country and in other countries. Nevertheless, some cultural information contained in the text might present points of conflict. The question is: what approach might a teacher take to these materials? One possibility, of course, is to omit the lesson. Gray (2000), for example, found that about half the teachers he surveyed would omit what they considered to be culturally inappropriate materials. Hyde (1994), on the other hand, argues strongly against the idea of censorship. He maintains that a better alternative would be to take an analytic path in which the cultural content is explicitly dealt with, 'drawing students' attention to their own history and culture, as well as to those of the target culture, in order to explain and contrast the difference' (p. 301–2). Hyde maintains that it is especially important to deal explicitly with cultural content in the case of the teaching of English since 'English is situated at the interface of foreign and native cultural values to a greater extent than any other language because of its greater use around the world' (p. 303).

How might the cultural elements in the lesson on garage sales then be dealt with explicitly so as to establish a sphere of interculturality and develop cross-cultural awareness? Obviously, this depends to a large extent on the dynamics of the particular classroom. If the teacher were from a culture that had garage sales, he or she might explain the meaning that they have for various people in the culture, highlighting the point made earlier that there would be a diversity of views. Hence, for some people, garage sales might be a way to save money, for some they might be a social activity, for some a diversion, and for others an unpleasant and avoided event. However, because the topic may be largely irrelevant for many Iranian students, what is the value of dealing with it? This again depends on the teacher's approach. One potentially productive approach would be to encourage students to consider their own culture in light of this event. Why do they think garage sales are not common in Iran, and that the household sales that do occur differ significantly both in what items are sold and how they are sold? Under what circumstances do Iranians seek advice and whom do they consult? In other words, the text could provide a context for students to compare elements of their own culture with another, helping them to arrive at a better understanding of both cultures.

A good deal of cultural information in ELT texts, however, is not innocuous. It often presents a western, middle-class life style in contexts that, as Prodromou (1988) puts it, are not only imaginary but also vacuous. Such materials can easily alienate learners as they marginalize the students' own experience. Canagarajah (1999b), in his in-depth study of English teaching in Sri Lanka, carefully documents the various ways students resist such marginalization by glossing texts with drawings and words that clearly illustrate their opposition. Our work in South Africa (Chick and McKay 2001) demonstrated that student opposition can be quite complex. Whereas in Canagarajah's research, students were often resisting elements of western culture, in our work we found examples of students positioning themselves within a western middle-class framework. For example, in one multi-ethnic South African high school, the teacher, who was white, introduced a poem, 'The Mantis', written by one of the first published South African women poets. The teacher pointed out that in the Zulu tradition there are many myths surrounding the mantis but when she asked one of the black girls to provide information about these myths, the girl described what 'they' believe, thus distancing herself from the community that holds these beliefs.

The linking of the English curriculum with largely middle-class western influenced values needs to be carefully considered in the context of EIL in which, as we have argued, one of the primary aims is to use English to explain one's own culture to others. Hence, it is important to approach all cultural content in EIL materials reflectively. One way this can be done is to consider the following questions in reference to specific cultural content.

1 Why is this topic being written about?
2 How is this topic being written about?
3 What other ways of writing about the topic are there?
   (Kress 1985: 7 as cited in Wallace 1992: 123)

Let us take, for example, the text on garage sales. If we consider why the topic was written about, the choice of content was perhaps made on the basis of student interest in a typical American event. However, the materials also have a clear language agenda. The context provides a basis for introducing the vocabulary of various household objects and for practicing expressions of asking for and giving advice. The juxtaposition of language agenda and cultural contents is a feature of many language texts. Unfortunately, this dual purpose often results in teachers focusing on the language agenda and leaving the cultural content largely un-processed.

As far as the second question, 'How is the topic being written about?', is concerned, students are presented with what appears to be a very objective account of garage sales. However, this kind of event reflects a variety of cultural assumptions.

For example, it might suggest that people have a variety of objects that they no longer want or need, including what for many would be luxuries (jewelry, a clock radio, a cassette recorder). Or it might also suggest that there is a value in buying items cheaply, and that people are willing to purchase used personal items like underwear and sheets. For some people, garage sales might provide a way to survive in a society in which goods are not equally distributed. For others, they might represent thrift and resourcefulness.

Finally, what other ways of writing about the topic are there? Any presentation of a topic should explore the various meanings that the event has for people in that culture and encourage students to reflect on the event in reference to their own culture. In order to establish a sphere of inter-culturality, so critical to the use of EIL, it is essential that the cultural information presented in a text be processed reflectively so that learners can explore cultural differences and gain greater insight into their own culture.

As was suggested earlier in the chapter, not only is the choice of the cultural content of teaching materials important in EIL, but also the way in which texts are developed and used in various domains. In order to address the latter role of culture, we turn now to an examination of discourse communities and the use of EIL for specific purposes.

The role of culture in discourse communities

Swales (1990) argues persuasively for the need to separate the notion of speech communities from discourse communities. He maintains that discourse communities are different from speech communities in that literacy 'takes away locality and parochiality' (1990: 24) since writers are more likely than speakers to communicate with members in distant places and react to writings from the past. Furthermore, whereas in many cases speech communities serve social needs, individuals who join discourse communities often do so to achieve functional objectives. Finally, and most importantly for our purposes, speech communities are

> centripetal (they tend to absorb people into that general fabric), whereas discourse communities are centrifugal (they tend to separate people into occupational or speciality-interest groups). A speech community typically inherits its membership by birth, accident or adoption; a discourse community recruits its members by persuasion, training or relevant qualification . . . an archetypal discourse community tends to be a *Specific Interest Group*.
> (Swales 1990: 24)

As was pointed out in Chapter 1, one of the major reasons for the spread of English is that it serves a vast array of specific purposes. Not only is it used to record a large amount of knowledge in a great variety of fields, but it is also used as the medium of communication in numerous international organizations, various modes of entertainment, trade, and diplomacy. Hence, English serves as the medium for countless discourse communities. In order to explore what this fact suggests for the teaching of EIL, it is important to consider more fully what is meant by a discourse community.

Swales contends that discourse communities share the following defining criteria:

> there are common goals, participatory mechanisms, information exchange, community specific genres, highly specialized terminology and a high level of expertise. On the other hand, distance between members geographically, ethnically and socially presumably means that they do not form a speech community.
> (Swales 1990: 29)

The rise of EIL, along with the development of new technology, has enabled the development of discourse communities that are geographically, ethnically, and socially quite diverse. EIL is essential to the existence of many of these specialized discourse communities; at the same time it is their growth that is fueling the spread of English. Indeed one of the major reasons many individuals have today for learning English is to join a discourse community. In terms of the teaching of EIL, what knowledge do individuals need to partake in one?

Obviously, they need expertise in the discourse community's field, knowledge that is generally acquired outside of an EIL classroom. They also need knowledge of the specialized lexicon of the field, an area that can be addressed in an EIL classroom. Finally, they need knowledge of the community specific genres. It is here that EIL classrooms can be most useful. For Swales (1990), genres are composed of a class of communicative events such as news items or academic papers that serve a particular communicative purpose. This purpose shapes the structure of the discourse in each genre, and influences the choice of content and style. How can learners acquire an understanding of the genres specific to the discourse community to which they want to belong?

Whereas some people contend that the acquisition of literacy is essentially an individual accomplishment (see McKay (1996) for a summary of this perspective), many today recognize the social and cultural basis of literacy. Gee (1990), for example, argues that literacy practices are always interwoven into larger social practices. He calls these practices Discourses, with a capital D, and defines them as 'ways of believing, interacting, valuing, thinking, believing, speaking, and often reading and writing that are accepted as instantiations of particular roles . . . by specific *groups of people*' (xix). Hence, for Gee and others, mastering the discourse of a specific community is not a matter of learning a particular set of rules, but rather involves a process of apprenticeship and enculturation into the social and cultural practices of a discourse community.

Let us take a specific example of a discourse community and consider some of the social and cultural knowledge that is needed to operate in it. Imagine a biochemist who belongs to an international English-medium professional organization that holds an annual convention to share research findings. In order to participate in such a conference, the biochemist might want to submit an abstract for a paper. In order to do this successfully, he or she would, of course, need to have an understanding of the genre 'paper abstract'. This would involve examining the linguistic and rhetorical structure of a variety of abstracts previously submitted to the conference. But in addition, he or she would need to be aware of how abstract submissions fit into the overall operation of the organization. Who reviews the abstracts, and what do they look for? Having this knowledge will enable the biochemist to frame his or her abstract in such a way that it will have a greater chance of being accepted. How can such knowledge of the larger sociocultural context be promoted in an EIL classroom?

Swales (1990) offers a valuable framework for promoting such knowledge. He contends that language-learning tasks for English for specific purposes should entail attention to the relevant discourse community itself, instructional materials, and genres. He maintains that in order for materials designers to understand a discourse community, it is important that they undertake ethnographic studies involving observations, participation, interviews, questionnaires, and so on. In other words, materials designers and educators need to be aware of how particular texts are used within the total social and cultural fabric of a discourse community. According to Swales, materials designers also need to examine existing instructional materials and evaluate them in reference to the way English is used within particular genres in actual discourse communities. Finally, they need to undertake a discourse analysis of various examples of a particular genre. Given this information, they can then design appropriate language-learning tasks.

What is important to note for our purposes is that the design of these tasks is informed by an understanding of how a particular literacy practice fits into the sociocultural context of a discourse community. However, as was noted at the beginning of the chapter, the cultural content in EIL pedagogy for specific discourse communities is quite different from the primary cultural content that we examined earlier in the chapter. Whereas in some EIL teaching contexts, it will be important to consider what primary (geographically and ethnically based) culture should provide the basis for the content of materials, in other contexts, where learning English is related to specific occupational or professional purposes, the cultural content will be informed by the sociocultural literacy practices of the discourse community.

The use of EIL within specific discourse communities, then, involves a different notion of culture than that discussed earlier in the chapter. The sociocultural knowledge that informs discourse communities is not tied to specific geographically and ethnically based cultures. Rather it is based on the social and cultural practices of a particular group of people who are brought together for specific purposes. Because the cultural basis of such specialized discourse communities is not directly connected with any particular primary culture, or cultures, but rather transcends geographical, social, and ethnic borders, these discourse communities are examples of an international community *par excellence*. Although the use of EIL should not be equated with English for specific purposes, it is the use of English for specific purposes that has the greatest potential for developing truly international communities.

Summary

In this chapter we have examined the role of culture in the teaching of EIL. We began by defining culture as the knowledge people have learned as members of their social group, emphasizing the notion that it is a social construct in which the meanings people have for the things around them are modified by their interaction with others. We argued that it is extremely important to recognize the diversity that exists within any culture, and we emphasized the importance of establishing a sphere of interculturality in EIL classrooms so that individuals gain insight into their own culture. These insights can then be shared in cross-cultural encounters undertaken in international contexts. We then considered the primary rationales offered for the inclusion of culture in language teaching: first, that culture is embedded in the language itself, particularly in the semantics of language; and second, that cultural content is motivating in language learning. We noted that some dispute the motivating influence of cultural content, particularly that of the target culture.

The question of which culture to include in EIL materials—the source culture, the target culture, or an international culture—was examined in the context of the cultural background of the students and the teacher. We emphasized that there are possible advantages to including each kind, depending on how the materials are approached. We highlighted three principles that should inform how cultural content is handled in an EIL classroom. First, the materials should be used in such a way that students are encouraged to reflect on their own culture in relation to others, thus helping to establish a sphere of interculturality. Second, the diversity that exists within all cultures should be emphasized. And finally, cultural content should be critically examined so that students consider what assumptions are present in the text and in what other ways the topic could be discussed. We ended the chapter by examining the way in which socio-cultural factors influence how language is used in specific discourse communities, and argued that the cultural basis of such communities is not that of geographical and ethnic characteristics but rather of shared interests. We turn now to an examination of the ways in which culture influences how EIL is taught.

Further reading

On culture in language teaching

Atkinson, D. 1999. 'TESOL and culture.' *TESOL Quarterly* 33/4: 625–54.

Kramsch, C. 1993. *Context and Culture in Language Teaching.* Oxford: Oxford University Press.

Kramsch, C. 1998. *Language and Culture.* Oxford: Oxford University Press.

Zamel, V. 1997. 'Toward a model of transculturation.' *TESOL Quarterly* 31/2: 341–52.

On cultural content in language materials

Adaskou, K., D. Britten, and **B. Fahsi.** 1990. 'Design decisions on the cultural content of a secondary English course for Morocco.' ELT *Journal* 44/1: 3–10.

Alptekin, C. 1993. 'Target-language culture in ELT materials.' ELT *Journal* 47/2: 136–43.

Cortazzi, M. and **L. Jin.** 1999. 'Cultural mirrors: materials and methods in the EFL classroom' in Hinkel, E. (ed.): *Culture in Second Language Teaching.* Cambridge: Cambridge University Press: 196–219.

McKay, S. L. 2001. 'Teaching English as an International Language: Implications for cultural materials in the classroom.' TESOL *Journal* Winter 2001: 7–11.

Prodromou, L. 1988. 'English as cultural action.' ELT *Journal* 42/2: 73–83.

Prodromou, L. 1992. 'What culture? Which culture?' ELT *Journal* 46/1: 39–50.

On discourse communities

Swales, J. M. 1990. *Genre Analysis.* Cambridge: Cambridge University Press.

5 TEACHING METHODS AND ENGLISH AS AN INTERNATIONAL LANGUAGE

The teaching of EIL today takes place in a wide variety of contexts: in Outer and Expanding Circle countries, in private and public institutions, with young children and adults, with monolingual and bilingual teachers. Although there is great diversity among these contexts, all of them share the goal of developing proficiency in the learning of an international language. This chapter will argue that just as bilingual users of English need no longer look to Inner Circle countries to provide target models of use, educators need no longer look to Inner Circle countries for target models in pedagogy. Rather, local educators need to take ownership of the teaching of EIL and design pedagogies that are appropriate to the local culture of learning.

In order to present this argument, the chapter begins by elaborating on the concept of a culture of learning, emphasizing that a good deal of current discussion on this concept reflects a received view of culture, a view which depicts countries and regions of the world as homogenous and unchanging entities. The chapter argues that this view of a culture of learning needs to be replaced with one that recognizes that individual classrooms within one culture can vary greatly in terms of the expected role of the teachers and students.

Next the chapter describes how the spread of English has brought with it the spread of communicative language teaching (CLT). CLT is often advocated because it is seen as a modern approach designed in Inner Circle countries, which, according to some language teaching theorists, should provide the target model for language pedagogy. We then examine the position of advocates and opponents of this view. The chapter ends with suggestions as to what principles should inform a pedagogy of an international language.

A culture of learning

Cortazzi and Jin (1996) refer to the culturally influenced aspects of a language classroom as a 'culture of learning'. They maintain that

> much behavior in language classrooms is set within a taken-for-granted framework of expectations, attitudes, values, and beliefs about what constitutes good learning, about how to teach or learn, whether and how to ask questions, what textbooks are for, and how language teaching relates to broader issues of the nature and purpose of education. In many classrooms both teachers and learners are unaware that such a culture of learning may be influencing the process of teaching and learning. A culture of learning is thus part of the hidden curriculum.
> (Cortazzi and Jin 1996: 169)

The literature on ELT methodology is filled with characterizations of the culture of learning of various countries. Typically such discussions provide generalizations regarding the typical roles of teachers and students as well as the nature of learning, and reflect a received view of culture in which a particular culture is seen as a homogenous entity related to a specific geographical region. China is one country for which there exist many such descriptions. Cortazzi and Jin (1996), for instance, maintain that Chinese children are socialized into a culture of learning in which there is a strong emphasis on memory, imitation, and repetitive practice. In the early years the importance of discipline and the significance of giving children necessary knowledge is stressed.

Descriptions of a particular culture of learning also frequently include a comparison of the culture with western cultures of learning. Cortazzi and Jin (1996), for example, compare how Chinese students view certain aspects of student behavior with how western teachers perceive them. For example, they maintain that while western teachers view volunteering in class as showing strong interest and activity on the part of the students, Chinese students often see this as showing off and preventing teacher talk. As far as group discussions are concerned, many western teachers view them as useful interaction and student-centered learning; however, many Chinese students regard them as a fruitless activity that should be replaced by the teacher giving facts and generalizations.

Flowerdew and Miller (1995) contrast Chinese and western approaches to academic lectures, maintaining that the differences that exist are due to Confucian in relation to western values. They summarize these differences in Table 5.1.

Japan is another country for which there are many descriptions of the culture of learning. Carson (1992), for example, characterizes the social

Table 5.1: Confucian and western values as they relate to academic lectures (from Flowerdew and Miller 1995: 348)

Confucian	Western
respect for authority of lecturer	lecturer valued as guide and facilitator
lecturer should not be questioned	lecturer is open to challenge
student motivated by family and pressure to excel	student motivated by desire for individual development
positive value placed on effacement and silence	positive value placed on self-expression of ideas
emphasis on group orientation to learning	emphasis on individual development and creativity in learning

aspects of schooling in Japan. She argues that because the acquisition of second language literacy is influenced by first language literacy learning, educators should consider how literacy is acquired in the first language in order to design appropriate methodologies. On the basis of existing studies of first language literacy learning in Japan, Carson summarizes the Japanese culture of learning in the following way.

> To summarize, becoming literate in this highly literate country means learning to read and write in the Japanese educational system which reflects the values of Japanese society: the importance of education (and literacy), the need to work hard to succeed, the inherent value of the group, and the primacy of shared social purpose. In this context language is understood as a medium for expressing social cohesion, and not primarily as a medium for individual expression. (Carson 1992: 42)

In reporting on Japanese students' reactions to their English teacher, who was from the US, Miller (1995) contrasts the communication styles of Japanese and Americans in terms of five distinctions, as shown in Table 5.2.

On the basis of classroom observations, LoCastro (1996) characterizes English language classes in Japan as teacher-fronted, teacher-centered, and generally employing a grammar-translation method. In general, class time consists primarily of teacher talk.

Ballard and Clanchy (1991) go even further, providing an overall contrast of Asian and Australian students in terms of their attitudes toward knowledge, and their learning approaches and strategies. They maintain that, typically, attitudes toward knowledge form a continuum that runs

Table 5.2: Communication styles of Japanese and Americans (adapted from Miller 1995: 42)

Japanese	Americans
low self-disclosure	high self-disclosure
group consciousness	individualism
consensus	autonomous decision making
self-restraint as listener	attentive feedback
orderly turn taking	floor competition

from conserving knowledge to extending knowledge. Whereas Asian students tend toward the conserving knowledge end, Australian students tend toward the extending knowledge end. In terms of learning approaches, they posit a continuum that runs from reproductive, through to analytic, to speculative approaches, with Asian students toward the reproductive end and Australian students toward the speculative end. Learning strategies then develop from these approaches, with memorization and imitation used in reproductive learning, critical thinking used in analytical learning, and a deliberate search for new possibilities and expectations in speculative learning.

Such descriptions of cultures of learning raise several problems. First, they mask the diversity that exists within any culture. Indeed, as was pointed out in Chapter 4, national identities are not monolithic; rather they differ by age, social class, and region. Second, in many instances characteristics that are attributed to a particular culture of learning are not supported by studies based on extensive classroom observation. Kubota (1999), for example, points to a large body of research on Japanese primary schools that shows that the Japanese pre-school and elementary curriculum does indeed promote creativity, original thinking, and self-expression. These findings clearly undermine the stereotypical images of Japanese education that includes only mechanical learning and a lack of individualism, creativity, and problem-solving skills.

Third, and most important in the teaching of an international language, is that such characterizations of cultures of learning, as in the majority of the descriptions cited above, often contrast a particular culture of learning with western cultures, resulting in ideas of otherness and foreignness. Kubota argues that 'labels that symbolize a cultural dichotomy serve to create and perpetuate, rather than reflect cultural difference' (1999: 16). She maintains that this 'construction of Otherness is part of the colonial discourse' in which colonizers construct an artificial view of the 'Other as being what the colonizer is not, as having negative qualities such as backwardness, opacity, and a lack of reason, constituting a depersonalized collectivity' (1999: 16–17).

Several of the descriptions cited above clearly suggest a less positive view of Asian cultures of learning than those of western cultures. For example, whereas the phrase, 'extending knowledge', used by Ballard and Clanchy in reference to western cultures, suggests that new knowledge is being developed, the phrase, 'conserving knowledge', used in reference to Asian cultures, suggests knowledge of the past. Hence, Asian cultures are presented as lagging behind western cultures. The comparison of various non-western cultures with western ones suggests that in some ways the latter are the standard and hence should provide the model for the teaching of English. However, in the teaching of an international language, bilingual users should be allowed to take ownership not only of the language but also of the methods used to teach it.

Although no one would deny that cultural differences do exist, Kubota believes it is essential that describing cultural differences is not viewed as an end in itself; rather educators must seek to understand how 'difference is produced, legitimated, and eliminated within unequal relations of power' (1999: 27). Unfortunately, a discourse of otherness in which particular cultures of learning, particularly non-western ones, are depicted as less productive than western ones underlies much of the discussion of CLT. In these discussions, CLT is often viewed as the ideal methodology for English language teaching; at the same time, some argue that CLT, while the most productive approach, is not feasible in many countries because the local culture of learning tends to promote mechanical learning and a lack of individualism and creative thinking.

The spread of English and communicative language teaching

The history of ELT is usually described as if one method followed another. Brown (1994), for example, describes how, in the nineteenth century, grammar-translation was the main method in language teaching, and was followed in the twentieth century by the direct method. He then describes how, in the 1940s and 1950s, audiolingualism became popular, and how the 1970s witnessed the rise of so-called 'alternative' methods, for example community language learning and suggestopedia. In his description, all of these methods were superseded by the present-day emphasis on communicative language teaching (CLT). Such a view of teaching methodology, especially in relation to the teaching of EIL, has several problems. First, such historical accounts of language teaching, to the extent that they are accurate, primarily reflect the history of language teaching in Inner Circle countries. Second, if one looks at ELT in a global context, it is clear that many methods now described in methodology texts as no longer being used, for example grammar-translation and audiolingualism, are still used in countries outside the Inner Circle. Finally, in many cases it would be difficult to characterize a particular classroom as using only one method.

The rise of CLT is often attributed to a discontent with audiolingualism with its behaviorist view of language learning and emphasis on linguistic form rather than meaning. In contrast, informed by Hymes's (1972) notion of communicative competence, the goal of CLT is to promote meaningful, appropriate language use. Today many educators contend that CLT is, and should be, the dominant approach in ELT. Brown (1994), for example, maintains that the generally accepted methodological norm in the field is CLT. He notes, however, that although CLT is generally accepted, there are numerous ways in which it is defined.

As a way of clarifying the various definitions of CLT it is helpful I believe to discuss it as a methodology in the sense this term is used by Richards and Rodgers (1985). They maintain that a method involves three interrelated levels: approach, design, and procedure. The first level, approach, defines the assumptions, beliefs, and theories about the nature of language and language learning that inform a method. The second level, design, clarifies the relationship between theories of the nature of language and language learning and the form and function of instructional materials and activities. Finally, procedure comprises the classroom techniques and practices that are the result of particular approaches and designs. Most people would agree that the approach that informs CLT is one in which the primary purpose of using language is to convey meaning in appropriate ways. Language learning, then, should encourage learners to use the target language in appropriate ways to convey meaning. Clearly, these principles could provide the basis for an appropriate pedagogy in many contexts. It is, however, the area of design in which the greatest controversy regarding the characteristics of CLT exists and where there is the greatest potential for the use of an inappropriate pedagogy for a particular context. In examining this controversy, it is useful to consider the distinction made by Holliday.

Holliday (1994) contends that there are essentially two versions of CLT. The first one, which he terms the 'weak version', was developed largely in private institutes, either in Inner Circle countries or sponsored by Inner Circle countries in other countries. He calls the methodologies which comprise this version BANA methods. (BANA stands for Britain, Australia, and North America.) In this version of CLT, Holliday argues that a high premium is placed on oral work and maximum student participation in group and pair work. What he terms the 'strong version', on the other hand, was developed in public education systems either in primary and secondary schools or in universities in Inner Circle countries. He terms the methodologies which comprise this version TESP, standing for tertiary, secondary, and primary. In the TESP version of CLT, the focus is on learning about how language works in discourse. Students carry out tasks which are designed to pose language problems that help them understand how a text is constructed. This version is considered to be communicative in the sense that students communicate with a text. They may work with one another to solve a language problem and use their mother tongue in talking about the text but must report their results in English. Holliday argues that the strong version of CLT may be more applicable to a wider range of teaching contexts, particularly in Outer and Expanding Circle countries, where there are fewer resources and where students may not have the same instrumental purposes for learning English as students enrolled in private language institutes. However it is the weak version that is generally referred to when educators talk of CLT.

What has led to the widespread promotion of the weak version of CLT as the most productive approach for teaching English? Tollefson (1991) suggests one reason. He argues that the spread of English is linked to what he terms the 'modernization theory'. According to this theory, 'Western societies provide the most effective model for "underdeveloped" societies attempting to reproduce the achievements of "industrialization"' (1991: 83). When applied to ELT teaching, in modernization theory, 'Western "experts" . . . are viewed as repositories of knowledge and skills who pass them on to elites who will run "modernized" institutions' (1991: 97). If, as Holliday points out, the weak version of CLT was developed largely in BANA institutes, then the spread of CLT is a clear example of modernization theory. So-called experts from Inner Circle developed countries have passed on their expertise regarding language teaching methodology to help modernize English language teaching in 'underdeveloped' countries.

Whereas what Tollefson terms the modernization theory may well be one factor that has led to the spread of CLT, such a view hides the complexity of the issue. Just as the idea of linguistic imperialism (see Chapter 1) can be challenged on the grounds that in many countries English has spread because of the tremendous interest in learning the language, so too in many cases CLT has spread not only because of the promotion of the approach by western specialists but also because educators in these countries have advocated its adoption. Japan is a case in point. In 1989 and 1990, the Japanese Ministry of Education released new guidelines for the study of foreign languages in junior and senior high schools. According to LoCastro (1996), one of the primary aims of the new curriculum was to require teachers to promote speaking and listening skills as a way of developing the communicative language ability of the students. Furthermore, teachers were to strive to adopt CLT methods in their classrooms. Many Japanese educational leaders support this change. Koike and Tanaka (1995), for example, maintain that whereas the grammar-translation method was effective in teaching aspects of foreign culture, it is time 'for a change from the traditional to the communication-centered approach to foreign language teaching' (1995: 23).

Korea is another country that is encouraging the use of CLT. Convinced that the grammatical syllabus does not develop students' communicative competence, in 1992, the Ministry of Education published a new curriculum which clearly stated that CLT should replace the audiolingual and translation methods currently used in the schools. According to Li (1998),

> In the new curricula, the goal of English teaching is 'to develop the learner's communicative competence in English through meaningful drills and communicative activities, such as games, with the aid of audio-visual equipment' (Development Committee 1992: 180). Students are to learn by means of authentic materials, such as newspapers, magazines, English news on the radio and English TV programs. The curricula reflect the belief that 'CLT is characterized by learner-centredness' (p. 181), and teachers are encouraged to organize materials based on students' needs.
> (Li 1998: 682)

Thus, in a variety of countries educational leaders have chosen to attempt to implement the use of CLT in the belief that this is the most modern and productive way to teach English.

A final factor that has clearly contributed to the spread of CLT is textbooks. Many current ELT textbooks published in Inner Circle countries encourage activities which support the weak version of CLT in that a premium is placed on oral activities in which students interact with classmates. Directions like the following are common:

Practice 1

Look at the vocabulary below. Decide with your partner if the qualities listed are good or bad and write them on the spaces provided. Think of more of your own and add them to the lists. Compare your lists with your classmates.

outgoing	greedy	shy	conceited
smart	strict	considerate	moody
aggressive	open-minded	honest	hardworking

   Good Qualities   *Bad Qualities*

Practice 2

Think of a famous entertainer or athlete and write the name below. Write down what you think he/she is like (four qualities). Then ask two classmates. Write down their answers in the space provided. Form a small group and discuss your results.

(Richards, Bycina, and Aldcorn 1995: 77)

To the degree that these books are sold outside of Inner Circle countries, they provide an initial impetus for the use of CLT and further demonstrate the power of Inner Circle countries to influence the methodology of Outer Circle countries.

However, textbooks published outside the Inner Circle can also reflect a CLT methodology, particularly when the Ministry of Education has encouraged this approach. For example, in Morocco, the Ministry of Education textbook for secondary schools (*Further Steps in English*) notes that the purpose of the book is to introduce communicative activities and to involve students in learning activities by means of such devices as role plays, discussion topics, and games. A teacher, of course, need not implement textbook activities in the manner designated in the text. However, the fact that the textbook specifies a way to undertake the activity creates an expectation among students—and teachers themselves—that this is the correct way. This expectation can carry even more weight in textbooks approved by the local Ministry of Education since teachers generally believe, and often rightly, that they must teach according to the instructions in the book if they hope to get a positive evaluation from supervisors.

The above discussion demonstrates that just as the Inner Circle is often looked to for target models of language use, it is also frequently looked to for methodology models. Whereas this dependency of Outer and Expanding Circle countries may in part be due to a type of 'pedagogical imperialism' on the part of Inner Circle educators, there is no question that, just as with the spread of English, an equally important factor in the spread of CLT has been its conscious selection on the part of local educators. The spread of CLT, however, as is the case with the spread of English, has not gone unchallenged.

Challenges to the use of communicative language teaching

One challenge to the use of CLT has come from educators in the Inner Circle who question its theoretical basis. Swan (1985a), for example, argues

that the so-called communicative revolution is, like many of the trends
in methodology that preceded it, nothing more than a dogma. As he
puts it,

> Along with its many virtues, the Communicative Approach un-
> fortunately has most of the typical vices of an intellectual revolution:
> it over-generalizes valid but limited insights until they become
> virtually meaningless; it makes exaggerated claims for the power and
> novelty of its doctrines; it misrepresents the currents of thought it has
> replaced; it is often characterized by serious intellectual confusion; it
> is choked with jargon.
> (Swan 1985a: 2)

He goes on to criticize CLT's distinction between meaning and use, its
teaching of skills and strategies, its reliance on a notional-functional
syllabus, its use of authentic materials, and its real life fallacy.

He is particularly critical of the fact that CLT does not recognize the
resources that students bring to the classroom, particularly their fluency in
another language in which they have already learned to use communication
skills and strategies. He maintains that

> As far as the British version of the Communicative Approach is
> concerned, students might as well not have mother tongues.
> Meanings, uses, and communication skills are treated as if they have
> to be learnt from scratch . . . Communicative methodology stresses
> the English-only approach to presentation and practice that is a
> prominent feature of the British EFL tradition.
> (Swan 1985a: 85)

There is no question that a basic tenet of CLT is that the use of the
mother tongue should be discouraged as much as possible. Such a tenet
ignores the productive ways in which the mother tongue can be used in
class, and is particularly inappropriate in an era when English is being
acquired primarily in bilingual contexts.

Other Inner Circle educators challenge the use of CLT on the grounds that
it is not a culturally sensitive methodology. Ellis (1996), for example,
argues that there are several aspects of CLT that make it 'unsuitable for Asian
learners and teachers' (p. 214). Among these is the importance that CLT
places on process as opposed to content and its emphasis on meaning over
form. He maintains that 'in the confusion between Eastern and Western
world-views, it is quite natural to fall into the trap of assigning one's own
hierarchy of goals and value orientation to our counterparts from the other
culture' (p. 216). He argues that there is a need to recognize the social
principles that underlie CLT and to strive to mediate these differences when
CLT is used in eastern contexts. Whereas such discussions reflect a

sensitivity regarding the appropriateness of particular methods to specific contexts, they nonetheless promote the kind of otherness referred to above in which the diversity within one culture is minimized and a culture as a whole is compared with another.

Perhaps the most serious challenge to the spread of CLT comes from teachers outside of the Inner Circle who question the appropriateness of the approach for their particular teaching context. One of the earliest studies which provides evidence of this challenge is a survey of Chinese university teachers undertaken by Burnaby and Sun (1989). The Chinese teachers in the study believed that whereas CLT would be appropriate for Chinese students who intended to go to English-speaking countries, an emphasis on reading and translation would best meet the needs of many English language learners in China. In addition, the teachers pointed out several factors that made the implementation of CLT difficult in China. First, many students believed that this approach would not help them to pass the traditional national examinations, which tended to be discrete-point, and structurally based. In addition, many students felt that some of the activities in CLT seemed more like games than serious learning. Furthermore, the large class size and limited resources and equipment made it difficult to implement group work and use authentic materials. The teachers themselves felt that having to develop content for each lesson based on students' interests and needs was extremely difficult because

> (a) they were not familiar with a large number of authentic texts and/or had limited access to such texts; (b) they had difficulty knowing appropriate cultural contexts for points; and (c) they could not rely on their intuition in the construction of language exercises. (Burnaby and Sun 1989: 228)

Such objections to using CLT reflect the marginalization of bilingual teachers of English, who are placed in a position in which they are often asked to use materials containing cultural information with which they are not familiar.

Li's (1998) interviews with Korean secondary school teachers on the difficulties involved in implementing CLT demonstrate similar problems. Li's study revealed three sources of difficulty in using CLT. The first comes from the educational system itself, in which large classes, grammar-based examinations, insufficient funding, and a lack of support for teacher education undermine the implementation of this approach. Second, the students' low English proficiency, lack of motivation for developing communicative competence, and resistance to class participation make it difficult to use CLT. Finally, the teachers believe that their own inadequacies contribute to the problem. They feel that their deficiency in spoken English and sociolinguistic competence, along with their lack of relevant training and limited time to develop materials, add to their difficulties. Clearly teachers' feelings of inadequacy are compounded by the fact that the current Ministry of Education guidelines promote the use of CLT. Li, however, argues that it is essential for Korean educators to look within their own context for approaches to teaching English rather than depending on western expertise. As he says,

> Rather than relying on expertise, methodology, and materials controlled and dispensed by Western ESL countries, EFL countries should strive to establish their own research contingents and encourage methods specialists and classroom teachers to develop language teaching methods that take into account the political, economic, social, and cultural factors and, most important of all, the EFL situations in the countries.
> (Li 1998: 698)

Medgyes, a Hungarian teacher educator, has various concerns about the implementation of CLT in his country, even though he has publicly advocated the approach in teacher education courses. His primary concern is the burden CLT places on teachers. For a start, teachers using this approach are encouraged to base the syllabus on students' needs and interests. Yet, as Medgyes points out, most Hungarian students, like many EFL students, study English for no obvious reason other than because they are required to do so. Hence, teachers face a group of students who often have very little motivation to use English and uncertain needs for the language in the future. Teachers are also asked to develop authentic communicative situations where real messages are exchanged. Hence, 'teachers have to create favourable conditions for such needs to arise and get expressed' (1986: 108). Creating such contexts is, of course, particularly difficult in monolingual EFL classes, in which students would naturally use their mother tongue to communicate in so-called 'real' interactions. In addition, teachers are asked to do away with textbooks and substitute them with a 'wide stock of flexible and authentic "supplementary" material' (ibid.: 110), an extremely difficult task to undertake in countries in which there is not a wealth of readily available English texts.

Given these difficulties, Medgyes contends that perhaps the only teachers who could attempt to implement CLT are the elite, who have had the opportunity to exchange ideas at conferences and 'on arriving home, . . . feel obliged to promulgate all the trendy thoughts they have picked up, never doubting that their message is true and will reach the general public' (ibid.: 111). He concludes he believes that what is needed are educators who work halfway between 'the zealots and the weary' (ibid.: 112), local educators who are well aware of the complexities of teaching English in local contexts.

Students as well as teachers have challenged the use of CLT. Shamim (1996), for example, describes her students' reactions to innovations in her Pakistani university class, designed to make it more learner centered and thus more in keeping with a CLT methodology. She explained her rationale for including more group work and discussions to her class, telling them that if they did not like the changes, they could discuss the problem and suggest other alternatives. She soon found that the students resisted the change from what had been primarily a lecture format. Often they would come to class not having done the assigned reading, requesting that the lecture format be followed instead. On one occasion they even decided to stay away from class. By the end of the semester Shamim found that she had to assume more and more authority in the classroom. As she points out, it is ironic that the non-threatening and relaxed atmosphere she was trying to create in her classroom had, in fact, become a potential source of tension and conflict.

Shamim comments that, in general, educational planners see the role of the teacher as significant in implementing changes in methodology while that of the learner is largely ignored. Rather, it is assumed that learners will accept any change. However, as she notes, once a teacher has assumed a new role in the classroom, students may feel that they too can assume new roles, roles that at times reflect their resistance to the change. As she puts it,

> The innovative methodology which I was trying to introduce required a major redefinition of the authority structure in the classroom and was largely incongruent, I realized later, with the culture of the community. The learners' anxiety about the stability of the roles and responsibilities in the classroom, on the one hand, and the disruption of the essential norms of behaviour in the well-established social order, on the other, proved to be a greater force than the proverbial authority of the teacher in the Pakistani classroom. Also, once the teacher broke the contract, as it were, by stepping out of her traditional role and changing the routine structure of the classroom event, this seemed to provide a sanction to the learners to indulge in forms of behaviour that would be termed deviant in the framework of a traditional classroom.
> (Shamim 1996: 113)

Shamim's experience is a vivid illustration of the kinds of problems that can arise when traditional classroom routines are challenged, and highlights the need to involve learners in any methodological innovations. It also exemplifies the delicate balance that exists between the roles of teachers and students, in which standard routines are developed, providing classroom participants with a sense of security as to how the learning process should proceed. Thus, there exists a variety of evidence to demonstrate that the adoption of CLT, an approach largely developed and promoted by Inner Circle countries, has not been successful in many EIL teaching contexts outside of the Inner Circle.

Toward an appropriate methodology for English as an international language

Just as the use of English today is embedded in a variety of local contexts, so too is the teaching of EIL. Every EIL classroom is influenced by various contextual factors. These include the political and social context (e.g. official language policies, the role of English in the society, economic resources appropriated to ELT, and linguistic and cultural attitudes toward EIL); the educational institution itself (e.g. its English teaching objectives, material resources, philosophy of learning, and class size); the teachers' background (e.g. their English training and philosophy of teaching); and the students' background (e.g. their age, previous exposure to English, and learning goals). However, each classroom is unique in the particular dynamics that exist among the participants in the lesson. Because of this, as Prabhu (1990) points out, there is no one best method, and no one method that is best for a particular context. Even though attempts have been made to specify the many variables that affect a particular classroom in order to specify an appropriate method, such procedures obscure the moment by moment decisions teachers make to encourage language learning. Hence, as Prabhu suggests, perhaps 'there is a factor more basic than the choice between methods, namely, teachers' subjective under-standing of the teaching they do' (1990: 172)—in other words, what Prabhu terms a teacher's 'sense of plausibility'.

This sense of plausibility is influenced by teachers' own experience in the past as learners, by their experience teaching, and by their exposure to one or more teaching methods. A method then, for Prabhu is 'a highly developed and highly articulated sense of plausibility' (ibid.: 175). Thus, 'the best method varies from one teacher to another, but only in the sense that it is best for each teacher to operate with his or her own sense of plausibility at any given time' (ibid.: 175–6). This teachers' sense of plausi-bility is nicely exemplified in an article by Kramsch and Sullivan (1996), describing the use of a CLT textbook (Soars and Soars: *Headway Inter-mediate*) in a university English class in Vietnam. In observing the teacher's use of these materials, Kramsch and Sullivan found that they were approached in creative ways that were most likely not envisioned by the authors but which did reflect the culture of learning of that particular classroom. In Vietnam, students in English classes stay together in the same group throughout their university career; hence, they come to know each other quite well. This situation, along with the fact that teachers are generally honored and respected, results in a culture of learning that, according to Kramsch and Sullivan, has three central characteristics: the notion of classroom-as-family, teacher-as-mentor, and language-learning-as-play.

These characteristics affected how the CLT textbook was used in this classroom. The materials were designed to be used in small group work, but Kramsch and Sullivan found that in many instances the topics were examined by the entire class with a language-as-family focus. For example, one specific lesson entitled, 'Vocabulary of character: What sort of person are you?' asked students to write 'Yes', 'No', or 'Sometimes' as they answered questions about their own behavior. In western contexts using a CLT approach, students would likely be asked first to answer the questions individually and then to get into small groups to discuss their responses. However, this is not what occurred in this Vietnamese classroom in which no time was allowed for individual response or group work. Rather the class as a whole went through the list, with individual students calling out their responses and other students commenting on these responses. Throughout the process there was a good deal of laughter as students called out their responses simultaneously. For example, in answer to the question, 'Do you frequently make people laugh?' the exchange was as follows.

> Ss   ((laugh)) [Yes.]
>   [Sometimes.]
> T   No. Always, OK.
> Ss   ((laugh))
> (Kramsch and Sullivan 1996: 204)

Hence, even though the textbook writers may have intended the book to be used in a particular way, this group of students and teacher had their own culture of learning, a culture undoubtedly affected by the larger Vietnamese culture and the institutional structure of the university, yet still unique because of the shared history of the individuals in the classroom.

The interaction in this Vietnamese class provides an illustration of how teachers have creatively adopted CLT textbooks to suit their particular teaching context. Many of the textbooks published today in Inner Circle countries reflect a methodology that might be characterized as what Holliday (1994) terms the weak version of CLT, in which a premium is put on student oral participation and an important measure of a 'good lesson' is the amount of student talk that occurs. This premium on student talk, coupled with the assumption in CLT that language learning is a social endeavor, results in a strong expectation that there will be group or pair work. Yet, as the example from Vietnam demonstrates, such an approach may not be in keeping with the local culture of learning. Indeed, since EIL educators are involved in teaching an international language that no longer belongs to any one nation or culture, then it is reasonable that the way in which this language is taught should not be linked to a particular culturally influenced methodology; rather the language should be taught in a manner consistent with local cultural expectations. In short, an appropriate EIL methodology presupposes sensitivity to the local cultural context in which local educators, on the basis of their sense of plausibility, determine what happens in the classroom. As Kramsch and Sullivan put it,

> appropriate pedagogy must also be a pedagogy of appropriation. The English language will enable students of English to do business with native and non-native speakers of English in the global world market and for that they need to master the grammar and vocabulary of standard English. But they also need to retain control of its use.
> (Kramsch and Sullivan 1996: 211)

For Kramsch and Sullivan, such a view of an appropriate pedagogy is in keeping with the political motto, 'Think globally, act locally', which, in language-teaching terms, might be translated as 'global thinking, local teaching' (p. 200). This motto is particularly important for the teaching of EIL. Clearly, EIL educators today need to recognize the use of English as a global language for a wide variety of cross-cultural communicative purposes. Yet in developing an appropriate pedagogy, they also need to consider how English is embedded in the local context.

As we have demonstrated in earlier chapters, the teaching of EIL takes place in a wide diversity of contexts. In some countries, for example Singapore, English is the medium of instruction. In other countries, for example Jamaica, students bring to the classroom their own distinct variety of English. In other countries, for example Japan, the learning of English in public schools is promoted through national examinations. In addition, the teaching of English in, for example, public versus private institutions and urban versus rural institutions tend to be quite different. In light of such diversity, it is naïve to assume that one method is best for all.

The promotion of CLT has been fueled by the tendency to extend the assumptions of Inner Circle countries about English language learning to other countries. It has also been supported by a large textbook industry that promotes communicative approaches. Unfortunately, the prevalent assumption that CLT is the best method for the teaching of EIL has several negative effects. It often requires students to become involved in language activities that challenge their notion of appropriate language behavior in a classroom. Its emphasis on an English-only classroom can undermine the productive use of the mother tongue in the learning of English, which is particularly problematic in an era in which English is being learned primarily in bilingual classrooms. Most importantly, it can marginalize local teachers, who at times are asked to implement a methodology that may be in conflict with their own sense of plausibility. Clearly the first step toward an appropriate methodology must be for local educators, as Kramsch and Sullivan argue, to be involved in a 'pedagogy of appropriation' in which they retain control of the teaching of English. As Canagarajah argues, 'If English teaching in *Periphery* communities is to be conducted in a socially responsible and politically empowering manner, the authority for conceiving and implementing the curriculum and pedagogy should be passed on to the local teachers themselves' (1999a: 90–1).

Clearly in the teaching of EIL, local educators should have control over how English is taught, implementing a methodology that is appropriate to the local context rather than looking to Inner Circle countries for models. However, this is not without its problems. For example, during a research visit to Chile in Fall 2000 on a Fulbright Scholarship, I found that currently local educators are attempting to develop a pedagogy that reflects their local context. Recently the Ministry of Education developed an English curriculum reform that gives primary emphasis to developing receptive skills. The program of study outlined by the Ministry specifies that 40 per cent of the English curriculum is to be devoted to developing reading comprehension, 40 per cent to listening comprehension, and 20 per cent to speaking and writing. The rationale given for this division is that for most Chileans, English will be used primarily to gather information through reading and listening rather than for speaking or writing. Many in-service teachers of English appear generally pleased with the overall design of the reform. Farias (2000), for example, in a survey of high school teachers in the Santiago area, found that 78 per cent of them support the objectives and content outlined.

Perhaps one of the main reasons for many in-service teachers' satisfaction with the reform is that all students in the state schools are given a textbook and cassette that implements the objectives specified by the Ministry of Education. The text, *Go for Chile* (Mugglestone, Elsworth, and Rose 1999), features a group of students from various countries who are on board a ship sailing along the coast of Chile on an educational cruise. This scenario enables the text to include themes which relate to both Chilean and international culture. The materials introduce academic topics by including texts and lectures on subjects such as climate conditions in various parts of Chile, and deal with learning skills like classification, brainstorming, and analysis. Hence, the texts, in keeping with the Ministry guidelines, strive to develop students' English language skills primarily in reference to their need to use English to access information in written texts and process academic lectures.

Whereas in general there appears to be support among in-service teachers of English for the objectives of the reform and the textbook, this support is less evident among pre-service teacher educators. At many universities involved in English education, there is minimal, if any, attention to the curriculum revisions mandated by the Ministry of Education. Some of the methodology instructors have not even seen the textbook *Go for Chile*. Others have expressed the opinion that teacher educators were in a better position to know what the students needed in terms of methodology than the Ministry of Education.

Those that espouse the development of a locally appropriate pedagogy argue that its design must be in the hands of local educators. What is not clear, however, is exactly what is meant by 'local educators'. One could argue that it is the individual classroom teacher who needs to define an appropriate pedagogy for his or her class. In many ways, this is reasonable. The individual classroom teacher, after all, is the one who knows the needs of the students, and must make the moment-by-moment decisions of classroom content and interaction in order to meet these. From another perspective, however, the classroom teacher needs support from the larger educational context to develop an appropriate pedagogy. In the case of Chile, the fact that high school students are provided with texts by the Ministry means that every child, regardless of economic background, has an English textbook and a cassette. Hence, one might argue that because a Ministry of Education has the resources to assess local English learning needs, to design appropriate materials, and to co-ordinate in-service teacher education programs, it is in the best position to determine what an appropriate pedagogy might be and to encourage this program among in-service and pre-service teachers. It could also be argued, however, that teacher educators are in the best position to encourage a locally sensitive pedagogy. Many teacher educators maintain that because they are aware of the most recent research and theory in English teaching, they are able to develop in future teachers the skills needed to design one.

Central, then, to the development of a locally appropriate pedagogy is the need to clarify exactly what is meant by local educators. Ideally all the key players of educational reform—the Ministry of Education, in-service teachers, teacher educators, and teachers in training—should be involved in the design of a locally appropriate pedagogy. Yet, as is evident in the case of Chile, co-ordination between these various players is difficult, with each group believing that they are the ones who are in the best position to make the decisions. Hence, although it is essential to recognize the importance of local educators being in control of the design of an appropriate pedagogy, particularly in relation to the teaching of an international language, it is equally important to recognize that local educators are composed of various interest groups, often having different and competing perspectives and agendas.

Summary

In this chapter we have argued that, as is the case with the spread of English, the choice of English teaching methodology should no longer be based on Inner Circle target models. We began by exploring the concept of a culture of learning. In keeping with Cortazzi and Jin's (1996) ideas, we defined a culture of learning as the taken-for-granted expectations about what constitutes good learning and good teaching. We described the characteristics that some attribute to the culture of learning of China and Japan, ending with a description of an overall contrast between Asian and western attitudes toward knowledge. We pointed out the dangers of such general descriptions of eastern and western cultures of learning, arguing that such an approach can perpetuate differences, promote the concept of otherness, and lead to simple dichotomies and stereotyping.

Next, we explored the spread of CLT, noting that many of the tenets of CLT reflect the characteristics that are often attributed to western cultures of learning, namely individualism, creativity, self-expression, and social interaction. We pointed out that one of the major impetuses behind the spread of CLT, as with the spread of English, is its association with modernization and westernization. This association has led educational leaders in many countries to promote the use of CLT on the grounds that this is the most effective way to develop language learning. Another major factor in the spread of CLT has been the development of communicative textbooks, often written in Inner Circle countries, but used in countries outside the Inner Circle.

Although there has been widespread support for CLT within most Inner Circle countries and by many educational leaders in other countries, there have also been challenges. Some educational leaders have questioned its theoretical basis, contending that proponents of the approach have made exaggerated claims for its power and novelty. Others have argued that CLT is not culturally sensitive in that it is not congruent with many eastern approaches to learning. The most serious challenge to CLT has come from teachers themselves, who feel that in many cases the approach does not meet their students' needs. In addition, some teachers believe that CLT makes unreasonable demands on their knowledge of western cultures, their fluency in the language, their planning time, and their textbook and material resources. Students, too, have challenged it, believing in some instances that CLT does not meet their learning needs and does not provide for the kind of teacher input they believe is valuable.

We ended by arguing that there is no one way of teaching that can meet all learning contexts of EIL today, nor is there a best method for each particular context. Rather, a key factor in determining an appropriate methodology is what Prabhu calls a teacher's sense of plausibility. We illustrated how local teachers are in the best position to know how to use materials in ways that are congruent with the local culture of learning and pointed out that an essential ingredient in the development of an appropriate pedagogy is for educators to have a global awareness coupled with local knowledge. In closing, we argued that rather than selecting methodologies that may marginalize local teachers, if the teaching of EIL is to take place in a socially responsible and appropriate manner, the control of the curriculum and method must be given to local teachers. We emphasized, however, that determining exactly what is meant by local control of teaching methods is problematic. In the final chapter we explore what goals and approaches need to inform the design of an appropriate pedagogy for the teaching of EIL.

Further reading

Descriptions and critiques of cultures of learning

Ballard, B. and **J. Clanchy.** 1991. 'Assessment by misconception: cultural influences and intellectual traditions' in Hamp-Lyons, L. (ed.): *Assessing Second Language Writing in Academic Contexts.* Norwood, NJ: Ablex: 19–36.

Cortazzi, M. and **L. Jin.** 1996. 'Cultures of learning: language classrooms in China' in Coleman, H. (ed.): *Society and the Language Classroom.* Cambridge: Cambridge University Press: 169–206.

Flowerdew, J. and **L. Miller.** 1995. 'On the notion of culture in second language lectures.' *TESOL Quarterly* 29/2: 345–74.

Kubota, R. 1999. 'Japanese culture constructed by discourses: implications for applied linguistic research and ELT.' *TESOL Quarterly* 33/1: 9–36.

Descriptions of CLT

Brumfit, C. 1984. *Communicative Methodology in Language Teaching.* Cambridge: Cambridge University Press.

Holliday, A. 1994. *Appropriate Methodology and Social Context.* Cambridge: Cambridge University Press.

Littlewood, W. 1981. *Communicative Language Teaching.* Cambridge: Cambridge University Press.

Critiques of CLT

Burnaby, B. and **Y. Sun.** 1989. 'Chinese teachers' views of western language teaching: context informs paradigms.' *TESOL Quarterly* 23/2: 219–38.

Ellis, G. 1996. 'How culturally appropriate is the communicative approach?' *ELT Journal* 50/3: 213–24.

Kramsch, C. and **P. Sullivan.** 1996. 'Appropriate pedagogy.' *ELT Journal* 50:199–212.

Li, D. 1998. '"It's always more difficult than you plan and imagine": teachers' perceived difficulties in introducing the communicative approach in South Korea.' *TESOL Quarterly* 32/4: 677–703.

Medgyes, P. 1986. 'Queries from a communicative teacher.' *ELT Journal* 40/2: 107–12.

Swan, M. 1985a. 'A critical look at the communicative approach (1).' *ELT Journal* 39/1: 2–12.

Swan, M. 1985b. 'A critical look at the communicative approach (2).' *ELT Journal* 39/2: 76–87.

CONCLUSION: RETHINKING GOALS AND APPROACHES

As we have seen, EIL is being taught today in a wide diversity of contexts, so, clearly, any sound pedagogy must be informed by a theory of language learning and teaching that is sufficiently complex to account for this diversity. As Prabhu (1990) points out,

> If the theories of language teaching . . . that we have at present fail to account sufficiently for the diversity in teaching contexts, we ought to try to develop a more general or comprehensive (and probably more abstract) theory to account for more of the diversity. (Prabhu 1990: 166)

What assumptions should inform a more comprehensive theory of the teaching and learning of EIL, and what goals and approaches follow from these assumptions?

Toward a comprehensive theory of teaching and learning English as an International Language

Three major assumptions should inform a comprehensive theory of the teaching and learning of EIL. These are related to language use in multi-lingual contexts, the promotion of native speaker models, and language variation. The spread of English has been caused both by speaker migration and by the macroacquisition of English by existing speech communities, although the increase in the number of bilingual users is largely the result of macroacquisition. This growing number of bilingual users suggests that a productive theory of EIL teaching and learning must recognize the various ways in which English is used within multilingual communities. Typically bilingual users of English have specific purposes for using the language.

Many of them use it to access the vast amount of information currently available in English, and also to contribute to this knowledge base. One purpose they all share, however, is the use of English as a language of wider communication in a global, and sometimes also in a local, sense. For this reason, cross-cultural encounters are a central feature of the use of EIL.

The second major assumption that should inform the teaching of EIL is that many bilingual users of English do not need or want to acquire native-like competence. (Such an assumption, of course, presupposes that there is some agreement as to what constitutes a native speaker, although, as we have demonstrated, this is clearly not the case.) Current theories of second language acquisition and pedagogy frequently posit that the goal of most learners of English is to develop 'native speaker' grammatical standards, phonological patterns, and discourse competence. There are, however, several reasons why many bilingual users of English may not see this as their goal. First, on a practical level they may not need to acquire the full range of registers that is needed by monolingual speakers of English since their use of the language may be largely restricted to formal domains. Second, there are attitudinal reasons why they may not want to acquire native-like competence, particularly in reference to pronunciation and pragmatics. Third, if, as we have argued throughout this book, EIL belongs to its users, there is no reason why some speakers should provide standards for others.

Finally, a theory of EIL teaching and learning must be informed by accounts of language variation based on linguistic rather than attitudinal factors. All linguistic systems are equal in the sense that they are rule governed. It is the association of specific linguistic systems with particular social groups that results in some varieties of a language being considered of more worth. Whereas it is important to recognize the social attitudes that are associated with particular varieties of English, it is also necessary to acknowledge that all varieties are fully adequate to serve particular communicative purposes. Hence, the varieties of English that have developed as a result of the spread of the language need to be recognized as appropriate and valid for particular domains. At the same time, the more access individuals have to the varieties spoken within their community, the wider the audience they can reach. Thus, the learning of relevant varieties of English, along with an understanding of their appropriate use, should be encouraged. A theory of EIL teaching and learning that fully recognizes the use of the language in multilingual contexts, acknowledges the equality of speakers, and also the varieties of English they use, suggests certain pedagogical goals.

Teaching goals for English as an International Language

To begin, the fact that the spread of English has, as is natural, brought with it language change and variation suggests that one goal of EIL teaching needs to be to ensure intelligibility among the speakers of English. In the teaching of EIL it is important to distinguish linguistic differences that create problems of intelligibility from those that may engender negative attitudes. For example, the pluralization of nouns like *equipments* and *evidences* will not cause problems of intelligibility; however, some may contend that such differences reflect a lack of competence on the part of the speaker and be an indication of the deterioration of the language. Clearly, in the teaching of EIL, educators want to strive to minimize the first type of differences. Hence, particular pronunciation and grammatical patterns and, in some cases, lexical innovations that cause problems in intelligibility need to be addressed. Language differences that do not cause intelligibility problems but reflect negative attitudes also need to be addressed but in a different manner. In this case the so-called lack of intelligibility results not from features of the language itself but from the social attitudes that surround particular linguistic features. Therefore, these kinds of differences need to be addressed in the context of language attitudes in which educators emphasize the fact that an international language belongs to all of its users and not exclusively to speakers of the Inner Circle. As speakers take ownership of English, they will likely change the language. Those changes that do not impede intelligibility should be recognized as one of natural consequences of the use of English as an international language.

A second teaching goal of EIL should be to help learners develop strategies to achieve *comity*—friendly relations—when English is used with speakers from other cultures. Speakers who use English within their own community have acquired a sense of appropriateness as to when and how to do so in this context. However, when they come to use the language for cross-cultural purposes, they may need to learn some aspects of pragmatic competence. Traditionally, the teaching of pragmatics for the use of English in such circumstances has assumed a 'native speaker' target. Yet, as we have argued throughout the book, native speaker models are inappropriate in the teaching of an international language, which by definition has become de-nationalized. Therefore, the goal in teaching pragmatics in EIL should not be to achieve native-like competence but rather to encourage the acquisition of interaction strategies that will promote comity. These strategies could include such things as developing ways to seek clarification, establish rapport, and minimize cultural differences. Teaching objectives should emphasize that pragmatic rules will differ cross-culturally, and be based on the assumption that these cross-cultural differences do not require speakers to acquire the pragmatic rules of another culture but rather to mutually seek ways to accommodate to diversity.

A final goal in the teaching of EIL should be to develop textual competence. One of the primary reasons for learning English today is to access and contribute to the large amount of information that is available in the language. This availability of information suggests that the primary goal of many learners will be to develop reading and writing skills. As in the case of pragmatic competence, the teaching goal of developing native-like textual competence needs to be carefully examined. Clearly, all EIL learners need to develop an awareness that cultural factors do play a role in rhetorical development and that those texts that conform to their own rhetorical patterns will be easier to process.

An important goal when teaching reading in EIL should be to encourage a view of it as an interactive process in which readers must take an active role in making sense of texts, particularly when the texts exemplify different rhetorical patterns from their own. Whether or not EIL learners also need to acquire knowledge of how to use particular rhetorical patterns in developing written texts depends on their specific academic and professional goals. To the extent that academic success in western contexts depends on the acquisition of western patterns of rhetorical development, bilingual users of English may want or need to acquire these. On the other hand, when written texts are designed primarily for a bilingual community within a country, the use of local rhetorical patterns is clearly appropriate.

Approaches to the teaching of English as an International Language

Approaches to the teaching of EIL need above all to be culturally sensitive to the diversity of contexts in which English is taught and used. In terms of materials, this suggests that the prevalent use of western cultural content in ELT texts needs to be examined. There are clear advantages to the use of source culture content as it minimizes the potential of marginalizing the values and lived experiences of the learners. Source culture content can also encourage learners to gain a deeper understanding of their own culture so that they can share these insights when using EIL with individuals from other cultures. Perhaps most significantly, source culture content does not place local teachers in the difficult position of trying to teach someone else's culture. The choice of cultural content is extremely important, but of equal importance is how the materials are used. To begin, all cultural content should be approached reflectively: learners should be encouraged to consider why the topic was chosen, how it is written about, and what other ways the topic could have been presented. In addition, it should be approached in such a way as to develop a sphere of interculturality, in which students learn about another culture as a basis for reflecting on their own.

Finally, EIL should be taught in a way that respects the local culture of learning. An understanding of the local culture of learning should not be based on stereotypes, or a received view of culture, in which assertions are made about traditional roles of teachers and students and approaches to learning, often in reference to western culture. Rather it should depend on an examination of particular classrooms. Although it is important to recognize that what happens in a specific classroom is influenced by political, social, and cultural factors that exist in the larger community, each classroom is unique in the way the learners and teacher interact with one another in the learning of English. Given the diversity of local cultures of learning, it is unrealistic to imagine that one method, such as CLT, will meet the needs of all learners. Rather, teachers must be given the right and the responsibility to employ methods that are culturally sensitive and productive.

The concept of thinking globally but acting locally is highly relevant to the teaching of EIL. The evidence clearly suggests that the use of EIL will continue to grow, an international language that belongs, not just to native speakers, but to all of its users. Given this shift in ownership, the time has come for decisions regarding teaching goals and approaches to be given to local educators so that they can take their rightful place as valid users of English. For, in the end, they are in the best position to understand what their students need to know, and to encourage them to learn and use English to fully participate in our growing global community.

GLOSSARY

Included in the glossary are terms that are central to a discussion of the teaching of English as an international language.

acrolect: In reference to EIL, this term describes a variety of English that has no significant differences from Standard English. This variety is often spoken by the most highly educated people and is used in published texts. (See *basilect* and *mesolect*.)

basilect: In reference to EIL, this term describes a variety of English that has significant grammatical differences from Standard English. This variety is often used by the less educated people of the society. (See *acrolect* and *mesolect*.)

bilingual users of English: Bilingual users of English are individuals who use English as their second language alongside one or more other languages they speak.

cline of bilingualism: In reference to EIL, this concept refers to the range of varieties of English spoken by individuals within one country, including everything from a market variety of English to an educated variety of English.

codeswitching: This term refers to the change of a language or a language variety by a speaker or writer. Such shifts in language or language variety can occur within a sentence or at a sentence boundary and can also occur when one speaker uses one language and the other speaker uses another.

codification: This term refers to the extent that particular features of a language are recognized in dictionaries, grammar books, and style guide sheets. Codification refers to the degree to which the use of a particular linguistic feature is sanctioned by the society.

comity: Comity entails attempts by a speaker to establish and maintain friendly relations with others in spoken encounters. It includes strategies that develop solidarity with and support for the listener.

comprehensibility: Comprehensibility refers to the ability to understand the meaning of a text. If listeners know that the word *salt* refers to a particular condiment, the word is comprehensible to them. (See *intelligibility* and *interpretability*.)

contrastive rhetoric: In reference to EIL, this is an area of research in second language composition that attempts to identify the different rhetorical patterns used by bilingual users of English. These patterns are then compared with typical rhetorical patterns used in Inner Circle countries.

discourse competence: This term describes the ability of a speaker or writer to develop a text that is cohesive and coherent.

Expanding Circle countries: This is a term coined by Braj Kachru to describe countries in which English is widely studied but has no official role. These include countries like China, Japan, and Germany.

illocutionary force: This is a term coined by J. L. Austin to describe the intended force of a particular utterance. The same form can have different illocutionary force. Thus, the sentence, 'What time is it?' could have the intention of opening a conversation or of hinting that one should leave.

Inner Circle countries: This is a term coined by Braj Kachru to describe countries that are English speaking.

intelligibility: In its narrow sense, this term refers to word-level recognition of a language. If listeners realize that they are listening to English words, then the language is intelligible to them. In its broader sense, it is also used to refer to comprehensibility and interpretability. (See *comprehensibility* and *interpretability*.)

interlanguage: This is a term coined by Larry Selinker to refer to uses of English made by learners of English that do not conform to Standard English patterns and represent learners' unsuccessful attempts to acquire the standard forms.

International English: International English is used by native speakers of English and bilingual users of English for cross-cultural communication. International English can be used both in a local sense between speakers of diverse cultures and languages within one country and in a global sense between speakers from different countries.

interpretability: Interpretability refers to the ability to understand the intent or purpose of a phrase. If an individual understands, for example, that the phrase, "Do you have any salt?" is a request for salt, then the language is interpretable. (See *comprehensibility* and *intelligibility*.)

language shift: This terms refers to the change from the dominant use of one language to another. Language shift often occurs among immigrants when they begin to use the language of their new country rather than the language of their homeland.

lingua franca: This term describes a language that is widely used by speakers of different languages to communicate. It can be an international language like English, a shared national language, or a pidgin or creole.

linguistic imperialism: This is a term coined by Robert Phillipson. Linguistic imperialism occurs when those in power establish a structural basis to promote the use of English, producing the dominance of English over other languages in the area.

mesolect: In reference to EIL, this term refers to a variety of English that has unique grammatical features that distinguish it from Standard English. (See *acrolect* and *basilect*.)

nativized variety: This term describes a variety of a language that has widely accepted phonological, grammatical, and lexical features that differ from other varieties of the language. In reference to English, such varieties often develop in Outer Circle countries where English is commonly used on a daily basis. They are also called *World Englishes*.

norm-dependent speech communities: This term, first used by Braj Kachru, describes speech communities that look to other speech communities for their language norms. Generally these are Expanding Circle countries.

norm-developing speech communities: This term, coined by Braj Kachru, describes speech communities that develop their own language norms through daily use of the language and codification. Generally these are Outer Circle countries.

norm-providing speech communities: This is a term coined by Braj Kachru to describe speech communities that provide language norms for other speech communities. Generally these are Inner Circle countries.

Outer Circle countries: This term, coined by Braj Kachru, describes countries in which English has a long history and serves a variety of functions in education, government, literature and popular culture. These include countries like India, the Philippines, and Singapore.

periphery countries: Periphery countries are non-core countries. They include both countries in which English has an official role along with one or more other languages (*Outer Circle* countries) and countries in which English has no official role (*Expanding Circle* countries).

pragmatic competence: This term refers to the ability of a speaker to use language that is appropriate for a specific context. This ability involves both knowing when a particular speech act like complimenting or apologizing is appropriate (sometimes referred to as sociopragmatic competence) and which linguistic form would be most appropriate to express this intention (often referred to as pragmalinguistic competence).

second language acquisition: This term refers to the process by which a speaker develops proficiency in another language.

Standard English: This term refers to the variety of English that is generally used in the printed media and carries the most prestige. Some contend that Standard English can be spoken with any accent.

world Englishes: These are varieties of English spoken in Outer Circle countries in which the widespread use of English has led to the development of particular standards of use. They are also called nativized varieties of English.

BIBLIOGRAPHY

Adaskou, K., D. Britten, and **B. Fahsi.** 1990. 'Design decisions on the cultural content of a secondary English course for Morocco.' *ELT Journal* 44/1:3–10.

Agnihotri, R. K. 1994. 'Sound patterns of Indian English: a sociolinguistic perspective' in Agnihotri, R. K. and A. L. Khanna (eds.): *Second Language Acquisition: Socio-Cultural and Linguistic Aspects of English in India.* New Delhi: Sage: 235–46.

Alptekin, C. 1993. 'Target-language culture in ELT materials.' *ELT Journal* 47/2: 136–43.

Aston, G. 1993. 'Notes on the interlanguage of comity' in Kasper, C. and S. Blum-Kulka (eds): *Interlanguage Pragmatics.* New York: Oxford University Press: 224–50.

Atkinson, D. 1999. 'TESOL and culture.' *TESOL Quarterly* 33/4: 625–54.

Bachman, L. 1990. *Fundamental Considerations in Language Testing.* Oxford: Oxford University Press.

Bailey, R. W. and **M. Gorlach** (eds). 1983. *English as a Global Language.* Ann Arbor: University of Michigan Press.

Bakhtin, M. M. 1981. *The Dialogic Imagination* (C. Emerson and M. Holquist, trans.; M. Holquist, ed.). Austin: University of Texas Press. (Original work published 1975.)

Ballard, B. and **J. Clanchy** 1991. 'Assessment by misconception: cultural influences and intellectual traditions' in Hamp-Lyons, L. (ed.): *Assessing Second Language Writing in Academic Contexts.* Norwood, NJ: Ablex: 19–36.

Bamgboṣe, A. 1992. 'Standard Nigerian English: issues of identification' in Kachru, B. B. (ed.): *The Other Tongue* Chicago: University of Illinois Press: 148–61.

Bamgboṣe, A. 1998. 'Torn between the norms: innovations in world Englishes.' *World Englishes* 17/1: 1–14.

Banjo, L. A. 1971. 'Towards a definition of "standard Nigerian spoken English"' in *Actes du 8e Congrès de la Société Linguistique de l'Afrique.* Abidjan: Université d'Abidjan: 165–75.

Bardovi-Harlig, K. and **Z. Dörnyei.** 1998. 'Do language learners recognize pragmatic violations? Pragmatic versus grammatical awareness in structured L2 learning.' *TESOL Quarterly* 32/2: 233–62.

Bickerton, D. 1975. *Dynamics of a Creole.* Cambridge: Cambridge University Press.

Bisong, J. 1995. 'Language choice and cultural imperialism: a Nigerian perspective.' *ELT Journal* 49/2: 122–32.

Bley-Vroman, R. W. 1983. 'The comparative fallacy in interlanguage studies: The case of systematicity.' *Language Learning* 33: 1–17.

Blum-Kulka, S., J. House, and **G. Kasper (eds).** 1989. *Cross-cultural Pragmatics: Requests and Apologies.* Norwood, NJ: Ablex.

Braine, G. (ed.). 1999. *Non-Native Educators in English Language Teaching.* Mahwah, NJ: Lawrence Erlbaum Associates.

Brown, G. 1990. 'Cultural values: the interpretation of discourse.' *ELT Journal* 44/1: 11–24.

Brown, H. D. 1986. 'Learning a second language' in Valdes, J. M. (ed.): *Culture Bound.* Cambridge: Cambridge University Press: 33–48.

Brown, H. D. 1994. *Teaching by Principles: An Interactive Approach to Language Pedagogy.* Englewood Cliffs, NJ: Prentice Hall Regents.

Brumfit, C. 1984. *Communicative Methodology in Language Teaching.* Cambridge: Cambridge University Press.

Brutt-Griffler, J. 1998. 'Conceptual questions in English as a world language: taking up an issue.' *World Englishes* 17/3: 381–92.

Brutt-Griffler, J. 2002. *World English: A Study of its Development.* Clevedon: Multilingual Matters.

Burnaby, B and **Y. Sun.** 1989. 'Chinese teachers' views of western language teaching: context informs paradigms.' *TESOL Quarterly* 23/2: 219–38.

Butler, S. 1996. 'World English in an Asian context: the Macquarie dictionary project'. *World Englishes* 15/3: 347–57.

Butler, S. 1999. 'A view on standards in South-East Asia.' *World Englishes* 18/2: 187–98.

Byram, M. 1998. 'Cultural identities in multilingual classrooms' in Cenoz, J. and F. Genesee (eds): *Beyond Bilingualism.* Clevedon: Multilingual Matters: 96–116.

Canagarajah, A. S. 1999a. 'Interrogating the "native speaker fallacy": non-linguistic roots, non-pedagogical results' in Braine, G. (ed.): *Non-Native Educators in English Language Teaching.* Mahwah, NJ: Lawrence Erlbaum Associates: 77–92.

Canagarajah, A. S. 1999b. *Resisting Linguistic Imperialism in English Teaching.* Oxford: Oxford University Press.

Carrell, P. 1984. 'The effects of rhetorical organization on ESL readers.' *TESOL Quarterly* 18/3: 441–69.

Carrell, P. 1985. 'Facilitating ESL reading by teaching text structure.' *TESOL Quarterly* 19/4: 727–52.

Carson, J. C. 1992. 'Becoming literate: first language influences.' *Journal of Second Language Writing* 1/1: 37–60.

Cheah, Y. M. 1998. 'Acquiring English literacy in Singapore classrooms' in Gopinathan, S., A. Pakir, H. W. Kam, and V. Saravanan (eds): *Language, Society and Education in Singapore* Singapore: Times Academic Press: 291–306.

Chew, P. G. L. 1999. 'Linguistic imperialism, globalism, and the English language.' *AILA Review* 13: 37–47.

Chick, K. 1996. 'Intercultural communication' in McKay, S. L. and N. H. Hornberger (eds): *Sociolinguistics and Language Teaching.* Cambridge: Cambridge University Press: 329–49.

Chick, K. and **S. L. McKay.** 2001. 'Teaching English in multiethnic schools in the Durban area: the promotion of multilingualism or monolingualism?' *South African Linguistics and Applied Language Studies* 19: 163-78.

Cohen, A. D. 1996. 'Speech acts' in McKay, S. L. and N. H. Hornberger (eds): *Sociolinguistics and Language Teaching.* Cambridge: Cambridge University Press: 383–420.

Coleman, H. (ed.). 1996. *Society and the Language Classroom.* Cambridge: Cambridge University Press.

Connor, U. 1996. *Contrastive Rhetoric: Cross-cultural Aspects of Second-Language Writing.* Cambridge: Cambridge University Press.

Cook, V. 1999. 'Going beyond the native speaker in language teaching.' *TESOL Quarterly* 33: 185–209.

Cortazzi, M. and **L. Jin.** 1996. 'Cultures of learning: language classrooms in China' in Coleman, H. (ed.): *Society and the Language Classroom.* Cambridge: Cambridge University Press: 169–206.

Cortazzi, M. and **L. Jin.** 1999. 'Cultural mirrors: materials and methods in the EFL classroom' in Hinkel, E. (ed.): *Culture in Second Language Teaching.* Cambridge: Cambridge University Press: 196–219.

Crismore, A., K. Ngeow, and **K.-S. Soo.** 1996. 'Attitudes toward English in Malaysia.' *World Englishes* 15/3: 319–35.

Crystal, D. 1987. *The Cambridge Encyclopedia of Language.* Cambridge: Cambridge University Press.

Crystal, D. 1997. *English as a Global Language.* Cambridge: Cambridge University Press.

Dalton, C. and **B. Seidlhofer.** 1994. *Pronunciation.* Oxford: Oxford University Press.

Dalton-Puffer, C., G. Kaltenboeck, and **U. Smit.** 1997. 'Learner attitudes and L2 pronunciation in Austria.' *World Englishes* 16/1: 115–28.

Davies, A. 1991. *The Native Speaker in Applied Linguistics.* Edinburgh: Edinburgh University Press.

Ellis, G. 1996. 'How culturally appropriate is the communicative approach?' *ELT Journal* 50/3: 213–24.

Farias, M. 2000. 'ELT teachers' reception of the school reform.' Paper presented at the 6th International Conference IATELF Chile, Santiago, Chile.

Firth, A. 1996. 'The discursive accomplishment of normality: on *lingua franca* English and conversation analysis.' *Journal of Pragmatics* 26/2: 237–59.

Flowerdew, J. and **L. Miller.** 1995. 'On the notion of culture in second language lectures.' *TESOL Quarterly* 29/2: 345–74.

Gee, J. P. 1990. *Social Linguistics and Literacies: Ideology in Discourses.* London: Taylor and Francis.

González, A. 1995. 'The cultural content in English as an international auxiliary language (EIAL): problems and issues' in Tickoo, M. L. (ed.): *Language and Culture in Multilingual Societies.* Singapore: SEAMEO Regional Language Centre: 54–63.

Gopinathan, S. 1997. 'Education and state development: lessons for the United States?' in Fishman, J., C. Ferguson, and J. Das Gupta (eds): *Language Problems in Developing Nations.* New York: John Wiley and Sons: 249–64.

Gopinathan, S. 1998. 'Language policy changes 1979–1997: politics and pedagogy' in Gopinathan, S., A. Pakir, H. W. Kam, and V. Saravanan (eds): *Language, Society and Education in Singapore.* Singapore: Times Academic Press: 19–44.

Govardhan, A. K., B. Nayar, and **R. Sheorey.** 1999. 'Do U.S. MATESOL programs prepare students to teach abroad?' *TESOL Quarterly* 33/1: 114–25.

Graddol, D. 1997. *The Future of English.* London: The British Council.

Graddol, D. 1999. 'The decline of the native speaker.' AILA *Review* 13: 57–68.

Gray, J. 2000. 'The ELT coursebook as cultural artefact: how teachers censor and adapt.' ELT *Journal* 54/3: 274–83.

Griffith, S. 1999. *Teaching English Abroad.* Oxford: Vacation Work.

Gupta, A. F. 1998. 'A framework for the analysis of Singapore English' in Gopinathan, S., A. Pakir, H. W. Kam, and V. Saravanan (eds): *Language, Society and Education in Singapore.* Singapore: Times Academic Press: 119–33.

Hinds, J. 1987. 'Reader versus writer responsibility: a new typology' in Connor, U. and R. Kaplan (eds): *Writing Across Languages: Analysis of L2 Text.* Reading, MA: Addison-Wesley: 141–52.

Holliday, A. 1994. *Appropriate Methodology and Social Context.* Cambridge: Cambridge University Press.

Hyde, M. 1994. 'The teaching of English in Morocco: the place of culture.' ELT *Journal* 48/4: 295–305.

Hymes, D. 1972. 'On communicative competence' in Pride, J. B. and J. Holmes (eds): *Sociolinguistics.* Harmondsworth: Penguin: 269–93.

Hynes, M. and **M. Baichman.** 1989. *Breaking the Ice.* New York: Longman.

Jenkins, J. 1998. 'Which pronunciation norms and models for English as an international language?' ELT *Journal* 52/2: 119–26.

Jenkins, J. 2000. *The Phonology of English as an International Language.* Oxford: Oxford University Press.

Kachru, B. B. 1985. 'Standards, codification and sociolinguistic realism: the English language in the outer circle' in Quirk, R. and H. G. Widdowson (eds): *English in the World: Teaching and Learning the Language and Literatures.* Cambridge: Cambridge University Press: 11–30.

Kachru, B. B. 1986. *The Alchemy of English.* Oxford: Pergamon Press.

Kachru, B. B. 1989. 'Teaching world Englishes.' *Indian Journal of Applied Linguistics,* 15/1: 85–95.

Kachru, B. B. (ed.): 1992. *The Other Tongue.* Chicago: University of Illinois Press.

Kachru, B. B. 1994. 'The speaking tree: a medium of plural canons' in Alatis, J. E. (ed.): *Educational Linguistics, Cross-Cultural Communications* *and Global Interdependence: Georgetown University Roundtable.* Washington DC: Georgetown University Press: 1–17.

Kachru, B. B. 1996. 'South Asian English: toward an identity in diaspora' in Baumgardner, R. J. (ed.): *South Asian English.* Chicago: University of Illinois Press: 1–28.

Kaplan, R. 1966. 'Cultural thought patterns in inter-cultural education.' *Language Learning* 16: 1–20.

Kasper, G. 1997. 'The role of pragmatics in language teacher education' in Bardovi-Harlig, K. and B. Hartford (eds): *Beyond Methods.* New York: McGraw-Hill Company: 113–41.

Kasper, G. and **K. R. Rose.** 1999. 'Pragmatics and SLA.' *Annual Review of Applied Linguistics* 19: 81–104.

Kern, R. 2000. *Literacy and Language Teaching.* Oxford: Oxford University Press.

Koike, I. and **H. Tanaka.** 1995. 'English in foreign language education policy in Japan: toward the twenty-first century.' *World Englishes* 14/1: 13–25.

Kramsch, C. 1993. *Context and Culture in Language Teaching.* Oxford: Oxford University Press.

Kramsch, C. 1998. *Language and Culture.* Oxford: Oxford University Press.

Kramsch, C. and **P. Sullivan.** 1996. 'Appropriate pedagogy.' *ELT Journal* 50: 199–212.

Krauss, M. 1992. 'The world's languages in crisis.' *Language* 68/1: 7–9.

Kress, G. 1985. *Linguistic Processes in Sociocultural Practice.* Oxford: Oxford Univeristy Press.

Kubota, R. 1998. 'Ideologies of English in Japan.' *World Englishes* 17/3: 295–306.

Kubota, R. 1999. 'Japanese culture constructed by discourses: implications for applied linguistic research and ELT.' *TESOL Quarterly* 33/1: 9–36.

Land, R. and **C. Whitley.** 1989. 'Evaluating second language essays in regular composition classes: toward a pluralistic U.S. rhetoric' in Johnson, D. and D. Roen (eds): *Richness in Writing.* New York: Longman: 284–93.

Leki, I. 1991 'Twenty-five years of contrastive rhetoric: text analysis and writing pedagogies.' *TESOL Quarterly* 25/1: 123–43.

Li, D. 1998. '"It's always more difficult than you plan and imagine": teachers' perceived difficulties in introducing the communicative approach in South Korea'. *TESOL Quarterly* 32/4: 677–703.

Lick, H. C. and L. Alsagoff. 1998. 'Is Singlish grammatical?: two notions of grammaticality' in Gopinathan, S., A. Pakir, H. W. Kam and V. Saravanan (eds): *Language, Society and Education in Singapore.* Singapore: Times Academic Press: 281–90.

Littlewood, W. 1981. *Communicative Language Teaching.* Cambridge: Cambridge University Press.

Liu, J. 1999. 'Nonnative-English-speaking professionals in TESOL.' *TESOL Quarterly,* 33/1: 85–102.

LoCastro, V. 1996. 'English language education in Japan' in Coleman, H. (ed.): *Society and the Language Classroom* Cambridge: Cambridge University Press: 40–58.

Lowenberg, P. 1986. 'Non-native varieties of English: nativization, norms and implications.' *Studies in Second Language Acquisition* 8: 1–18.

Martin, R. 2000 'Temple University Japan, summer seminar project assignment', unpublished manuscript.

McKay, S. L. 1992. *Teaching English Overseas: An Introduction.* Oxford: Oxford University Press.

McKay, S. L. 1996. 'Literacy and literacies' in McKay, S. L. and N. H. Hornberger (eds): *Sociolinguistics and Language Teaching.* Cambridge: Cambridge University Press: 421–45.

McKay, S. L. 2000a. 'The challenges of developing multiliteracies in an era of globalization: a focus on South African and Singaporean language-in-education policies' in Brown, A. (ed.): *English in Southeast Asia 99: Proceedings of the Fourth English in Southeast Asia Conference.* Singapore: National Institute of Education: 21–31.

McKay, S. L. 2000b. 'An investigation of five Japanese English teachers' reflection on their U.S. MATESOL practicum experience.' *JALT Journal* 22/1: 46–68.

McKay, S. L. 2001. 'Teaching English as an International Language: Implications for cultural materials in the classroom.' *TESOL Journal* Winter 2001: 7–11.

Medgyes, P. 1986. 'Queries from a communicative teacher.' *ELT Journal* 40/2: 107–12.

Medgyes, P. 1992. 'Native or non-native: who's worth more?' *ELT Journal* 46/4: 340–9.

Medgyes, P. 1994. *The Non-Native Teacher.* Hong Kong: Macmillan Publishers, Inc.

Miller, T. 1995. 'Japanese learners' reactions to communicative English lessons'. *JALT Journal* 17/1: 31–53.

Mugglestone, P., S. Elsworth, and **J. Rose.** 1999. *Go for Chile, Book 1.* Santiago, Chile: Addison Wesley Longman.

Myers-Scotton, C. 1993. *Social Motivations for Codeswitching.* Oxford: Clarendon Press.

Ngũgĩ, W. T. 1986. *Decolonizing the Mind: The Politics of Language in African Literature.* Portsmouth, NH: Heinemann.

Nunan, D. 1991. 'Communicative tasks and the language curriculum.' *TESOL Quarterly* 25/2: 279–95.

Pakir, A. 1998. 'English in Singapore: the codification of competing norms' in Gopinathan, S., A. Pakir, H. W. Kam and V. Saravanan (eds): *Language, Society and Education in Singapore.* Singapore: Times Academic Press: 63–84.

Pakir, A. 1999. 'Connecting with English in the context of internationalism.' *TESOL Quarterly* 33: 103–12.

Pandey, P. 1994. 'On a description of the phonology of Indian English' in Agnihotri, R. K. and A. L. Khanna (eds): *Second Language Acquisition: Socio-Cultural and Linguistic Aspects of English in India.* New Delhi: Sage: 198–207.

Pandit, P. B. 1978. 'Language and identity: the Punjabi language in Delhi' in B. B. Kachru and S. N. Sridhar (eds): *Aspects of Sociolinguistics in South Asia.* Special issue of *International Journal of the Sociology of Language* 16: 98–108.

Parasher, S. V. 1994. 'Indian English: certain grammatical, lexical and stylistic features' in Angihotri, R. K and A. L. Khanna (eds): *Second Language Acquisition: Socio-Cultural and Linguistic Aspects of English in India.* New Delhi: Sage Publications: 145–64.

Paulston, C. B. 1992. *Sociolinguistic Perspectives on Bilingual Education.* Clevedon: Multilingual Matters.

Pennycook, A. 1995. 'English in the world/The world in English' in Tollefson, J. W. (ed.): *Power and Inequality in Language Education.* Cambridge: Cambridge University Press: 34–58.

Phillipson, R. 1992. *Linguistic Imperialism.* Oxford: Oxford University Press.

Prabhu, N. S. 1990. 'There is no best method—why?' *TESOL Quarterly* 24/2: 161–76.

Pride, J. B. (ed.). 1982. *New Englishes*. Rowley, MA: Newbury House Publishers.

Prodromou, L. 1988. 'English as cultural action.' *ELT Journal* 42/2: 73–83.

Prodromou, L. 1992. 'What culture? Which culture?' *ELT Journal* 46/1: 39–50.

Quirk, R. 1985. 'The English language in a global context' in Quirk, R. and H. G. Widdowson (eds): *English in the World: Teaching and Learning the Language and Literatures*. Cambridge: Cambridge University Press: 1–6.

Quirk, R. 1990. 'What is standard English?', in Quirk, R. and G. Stein (eds): *English in Use*. London: Longman: 112–25.

Quirk, R. and **Widdowson, H. G.** 1985. *English in the World: Teaching and Learning the Language and Literatures*. Cambridge: Cambridge University Press.

Ram, A. 1983. *Interviews with Indian Writers*. Calcutta: Writers Workshop.

Ramanthan, V. 1999. '"English is here to stay": a critical look at institutional and educational practices in India.' *TESOL Quarterly* 33/2: 211–31.

Rampton, M. B. H. 1990. 'Displacing the native speaker: expertise, affiliation, and inheritance.' *ELT Journal* 44: 97–101.

Rao, R. 1978. 'The caste of English' in C. D. Narasimhaiah: *Awakened Conscience: Studies in Commonwealth Literature*. Delhi: Sterling: 420–22.

Reid, J. 1994. 'Responding to ESL students' texts: the myths of appropriation.' *TESOL Quarterly* 28/2: 273–92.

Richards, J., D. Bycina, and **S. Aldcorn.** 1995. *New Person to Person: Communicative Speaking and Listening Skills (Student book 2)*. Oxford: Oxford University Press.

Richards, J., J. Platt, and **H. Weber.** 1985. *Longman Dictionary of Applied Linguistics*. London: Longman.

Richards, J., and T. Rodgers. 1985. 'Method: approach, design, and procedure' in Richards, J. (ed.): *The Context of Language Teaching*. Cambridge: Cambridge University Press: 16–32.

Richards, J. C. 1995. 'Easier said than done: an insider's account of a textbook project' in Hidalgo, A., D. Hall, and G. Jacobs (eds): *Getting Started: Materials Writers on Materials Writing*. Singapore: SEAMEO Regional Language Centre: 95–135.

Schaefer, R. P. and **F. O. Egbokhare.** 1999. 'English and the pace of endangerment in Nigeria.' *World Englishes* 18/3: 381–91.

Seidlhofer, B. 1999. 'Double standards: teacher education in the expanding circle.' *World Englishes* 18/2: 233–45.

Selinker, L. 1992. *Rediscovering Interlanguage.* London: Longman.

Shamim, F. 1996. 'Learner resistance to innovation in classroom methodology', in Coleman, H. (ed.): *Society and the Language Classroom.* Cambridge: Cambridge University Press: 105–22.

Shastri, S. V. 1996. 'Using computer corpora in the description of language with special reference to complementation in Indian English' in Baumgardner, R. J. (ed.): *South Asian English.* Chicago: University of Illinois Press: 70–81.

Shaw, W. D. 1983. 'Asian student attitudes towards English' in Smith, L. (ed.): *Readings in English as an International Language.* Oxford: Pergamon: 21–34.

Smith, L. 1976. 'English as an international auxiliary language.' RELC *Journal* 7/2: 38–43.

Spradley, J. P. 1980, *Participant Observation.* New York: Holt, Rinehart and Winston.

Sridhar, K. K. 1996a. 'Societal multilingualism', in McKay, S. L. and N. H. Hornberger (eds): *Sociolinguistics and Language Teaching.* Cambridge: Cambridge University Press: 47–71.

Sridhar, K. K. 1996b. 'The pragmatics of South Asian English' in Baumgardner, R. J. (ed.): *South Asian English.* Chicago: University of Illinois Press: 141–57.

Sridhar, S. N. 1996. 'Toward a syntax of South Asian English: defining the lectal range' in Baumgardner, R. J. (ed.): *South Asian English.* Chicago: University of Illinois Press: 55–69.

Sridhar, S. N. and **K. K. Sridhar.** 1994. 'Indigenized Englishes as second languages: toward a functional theory of second language acquisition in multilingual contexts' in Agnihotri, R. K. and A. L. Khanna (eds): *Second Language Acquisition: Socio-Cultural and Linguistic Aspects of English in India.* London: Sage Publications: 41–63.

Stern, H. H. 1983. *Fundamental Concepts of Language Teaching.* Oxford: Oxford University Press.

Strevens, P. 1983. 'What is "standard English"?', in Smith, L. (ed.): *Readings in English as an International Language.* Oxford: Pergamon Press: 87–93.

Svalberg, A. 1998. 'Nativization in Brunei English: deviation vs. standard.' *World Englishes* 17/3: 325–44.

Swales, J. M. 1990. *Genre Analysis*. Cambridge: Cambridge University Press.

Swan, M. 1985a. 'A critical look at the communicative approach (1).' *ELT Journal* 39/1: 2–12.

Swan, M. 1985b. 'A critical look at the communicative approach (2).' *ELT Journal* 39/2: 76–87.

Swerdlow, J. L. 1999. 'Global village', *National Geographic* 196/2: 2–6.

Tang, C. 1997. 'On the power and status of nonnative ESL teachers.' *TESOL Quarterly* 31/3: 577–83.

Tay, M. 1982. 'The uses, users, and features of English in Singapore' in Pride, J. B. (ed.): *New Englishes*. Rowley, MA: Newbury House: 51–72.

Thomas, J. 1995. *Meaning in Interaction: An Introduction to Pragmatics*. London: Longman.

Thomas, J. 1999. 'Voices from the periphery: non-native teachers and issues of credibility' in Braine, G. (ed.): *Non-Native Educators in English Language Teaching*, Mahwah, NJ: Lawrence Erlbaum Associates: 5–14.

Tollefson, J. W. 1991. *Planning Language, Planning Inequality*. London: Longman.

Valdes, J. M. (ed.) 1986. *Culture Bound*. Cambridge: Cambridge University Press.

Veltman, C. 2000. 'The American linguistic mosaic: understanding language shift in the United States', in McKay, S. L. and S. C. Wong (eds): *New Immigrants in the United States: Readings for Second Language Educators*. Cambridge: Cambridge University Press: 58–94.

Wallace, C. 1992. *Reading*. Oxford: Oxford University Press.

Widdowson, H. G. 1994. 'The ownership of English.' *TESOL Quarterly* 28: 377–88.

Widdowson, H. G. 1997. 'EIL, ESL, EFL: global issues and local interests.' *World Englishes* 16/1: 135–46.

Zamel, V. 1997. 'Toward a model of transculturation.' *TESOL Quarterly* 31/2: 341–52.

Zentella, A. C. 2000. 'Puerto Ricans in the United States: confronting the linguistic repercussions of colonialism' in McKay, S. L. and S. C. Wong (eds): *New Immigrants in the United States: Reading for Second Language Educators* Cambridge: Cambridge University Press: 137–64.

INDEX

Page references followed by g refer to entries in the glossary